*New Century
Vest-Pocket
Secretary's
Handbook*

Companion *Vest-Pocket* titles

- **Webster's Dictionary**

- **50,000 Words Divided and Spelled**

New Century Vest-Pocket Secretary's Handbook

MARY A. De VRIES

New Century Publishers, Inc.

Design Karen Yops

Copyright ©1980 by New Century Publishers Inc.
a subsidiary of New Century Education
Corporation.

Printing Code
13   14   15   16   17

Library of Congress Catalog
Card Number: 82-81063

ISBN 0-8329-1342-1

Printed in the United States of America

Contents

Preface   17

*THE SUCCESSFUL
SECRETARY*   19

    Personal Qualities   19
    Principal Duties   22
    Business Etiquette   26
    Business Relationships   29

1. MAKING TELEPHONE
AND VISITOR
CONTACTS   33

    *Receiving Callers at the
Office*   34

    Greeting Visitors   34
    Determining the Reason
    for the Visit   36
    The Caller Who Must Wait   37
    Callers with and without
    Appointments   38
    Announcing and
    Introducing Visitors   39
    Referring a Caller
    Elsewhere   40

Handling a Difficult Caller 41

Making Telephone Contacts 42

Telephone Courtesy 43
Answering the Telephone and Transferring Calls 44
Screening Incoming Calls 45
Placing Local and Long-Distance Calls 47
Handling Problems 48

2. HANDLING INCOMING AND OUTGOING MAIL 49

How to Process Incoming Mail 50

Opening and Sorting the Mail 50
Preparing and Routing the Mail 52
When Your Employer Is Away 54
How to Treat Different Classes of Mail 56

How to Prepare Outgoing Mail 58

Using Effective Mailing Techniques 58
Getting Signatures on Outgoing Mail 60
Assembling the Mail and Handling Enclosures 62

Folding and Inserting the
  Mail   64

*Important Postal
Information*   65

  Domestic Postal Service   66
  International Postal Service   72

3. USING TELEPHONE
   AND TELEGRAPH
   SERVICES   76

Major Telephone Services   77

  Station-to-Station and
    Person-to-Person Calls   77
  International Direct-
    Distance Dialing (IDDD)   79
  Mobile and Marine Calls   80
  Conference, Appointment,
    and Messenger Calls   81
  Equipment and
    Convenience Aids   82
  The Telephone Directory   84
  Special Services for
    Business   85

*Principal Telegraph
Services*   86

  Domestic Service   86
  International Service   88
  How to Count Charges   89
  How to Type Messages   91
  Tips on Cost Control   93

4. APPLYING TYPING AND DICTATION TECHNIQUES   95

Developing Successful Typing Techniques   96

Organizing Your Material   96
How to Make Special Characters   98
Typing on Forms and Ruled Lines   99
Handling Cards, Labels, and Envelopes   100
Typing Numbers and Fractions   101
Making Vertical and Horizontal Rules   103
Feeding Numerous Sheets   104
Making Carbon Copies   105
Making Corrections   107
Typing Stencils and Masters   108
Spacing After Punctuation Marks   110
Typing Reports and Tables   111
Preparing Material for Printing   113

Handling Dictation and Transcription   115

Tips on Taking Dictation   116
How to Transcribe Notes   117
How to Transcribe from a Machine   118

5. STREAMLINING FILING AND REMINDER SYSTEMS 120

How to Use Effective Reminder Systems 121

Using Calendars for Reminders 121
How to Set Up a Follow-up System 123
Using Tickler Card Files 124

How to Apply Effective Filing Techniques 125

Types of Filing Systems 125
Indexing and Alphabetizing Procedures 127
Containers and Equipment 129
Preparing Material for Filing 129
Cross-Referencing 130
Control of Material Taken Out 132
Record Retention and Disposal 133
Advanced Storage and Retrieval Methods 133

How to Handle Purchasing and Storage 135

Ordering and Requisitioning Supplies 135
Distributing Supplies 136
Storing Supplies 137

6. **IMPROVING OFFICE EFFICIENCY AND ORGANIZATION**   139

Establishing Better Procedures   140

    Planning and Organizing Your Work Load   140
    Using Shortcuts to Increase Efficiency   141
    Improving the Office Layout   143
    Using Forms to Save Time   144

Using Equipment to Increase Efficiency   145

    Electric, Automated, and Electronic Typewriters   146
    Dictation-Transcription Machines   147
    Calculators and Computers   148
    Addressing and Mailing Equipment   148
    Copying and Duplicating Equipment   149
    Information Storage and Retrieval Systems   150
    Miscellaneous Office Aids   151

7. **ARRANGING MEETINGS AND MAKING TRAVEL PLANS**   153

How to Handle Preparations for a Meeting   154

    Preparing for the Meeting   154

Special Duties During the
Meeting   157
Taking and Typing the
Minutes   159

*How to Make Travel
Arrangements*   161

Making Reservations   162
Preparing the Itinerary   164
Handling Foreign Travel   166
Traveling with Your
Employer   168

8. LEARNING TO WRITE
CORRECTLY   171

Using Proper Punctuation   172

Apostrophe   172
Brackets   173
Colon   174
Comma   175
Dash   176
Ellipses   177
Exclamation Point   178
Hyphen   178
Leaders   179
Parentheses   180
Period   181
Question Mark   182
Quotation Marks   183
Semicolon   184

*Learning Correct Spelling
and Word Division*   185

Basic Spelling Rules   185
Rules for Dividing Words   187
Troublesome Words   189

*Mastering the Basic Rules
of Capitalization*   190

  Abbreviations   191
  Educational References   192
  Geographical Terms   193
  Governmental-Political
   Terms   194
  Historical Terms   195
  Holidays and Seasons   195
  Judiciary   196
  Legislation   197
  Military Services   198
  Numbers   198
  Organizations   199
  Quotations   200
  Religious References   200
  Titles   201
  Trade Names   202

9. **USING CURRENT
  LETTER-WRITING
  PRACTICES**   203

Setting Up the Letter   204

  Attention Line   204
  Blind Carbon-Copy
   Notation   205
  Body   206
  Carbon-Copy Notation   207
  Complimentary Close   207
  Dateline   208
  Enclosure Notation   209
  Envelope   209
  Identification Line   210
  Inside Address   211

Mail-Instruction Placement 212
Personal Notation 212
Postscript 212
Reference Line 213
Salutation 214
Second-Page Heading 214
Signature 215
Subject Line 217

Selecting Letter and Memo Formats 217

Full-Block Letter 218
Block Letter 218
Semiblock Letter 219
Official Style 219
Simplified Style 220
The Memo 221

Using the Correct Forms of Address 222

Personal Titles 222
Professional Titles 223
Honorific Titles 224

Composing Letters and Memos 224

Writing for Your Own and Other Signatures 225
Whether to Use a Letter or Memo 226
Improving Your Skills in Composition 227

Model Letters and Memos 228

Acknowledgment 228
Apology 229
Appointment 229

Appreciation 229
Collection 230
Complaint 230
Confirmation 230
Follow-up 231
Introduction 231
Invitation—Informal 232
Invitation—Informal Reply 232
Invitation—Formal 232
Invitation—Formal Reply 233
Order 233
Request 234
Reservation 234
Sympathy 235
Thank You 235

10. KEEPING ESSENTIAL
    RECORDS 236

How to Keep Tax Records 237

Recording Expenditures 237
Recording Income 240

*How to Keep General
Financial Records* 243

Securities Transactions 243
Bank Account Transactions 246
Family Financial Matters 250

*How to Keep Insurance
Records* 252

Life and Health Insurance
Records 253
Property Insurance
Records 254

11. FINDING USEFUL
INFORMATION
SOURCES   257

   Organizations   258

      Government Agencies   259
      Trade and Professional
        Associations   260
      Colleges, Universities, and
        Trade Schools   261
      Research Institutes   263
      Local Clubs and Civic
        Groups   264

   Publications   264

      Dictionaries   266
      Encyclopedias   266
      Almanacs and Yearbooks   267
      Atlases   267
      Directories and Indexes   268
      Newspapers and
        Periodicals   270
      Biographical References   271
      Style and Word-Usage
        Books   272
      Books of Quotations   272
      Industry and Financial
        Information   273
      Governmental Data   274

GUIDE TO
MISCELLANEOUS DATA   276

      Two-Letter Postal
        Abbreviations   276
      Area Codes and Standard
        Time Zones   278

Proofreader Marks 280
Correct Forms of Address 281
Abbreviated Titles and
  Degrees 314
Common Abbreviations 319
Common Weights and
  Measures 330
Metric Weights and
  Measures 334
Metric and Common
  Equivalents 336
Mathematical Signs and
  Symbols 341
Common Percents and
  Fractional Equivalents 342

Index 343

Preface

The old adage that the best things come in small packages has merit when you consider the *New Century Vest-Pocket Secretary's Handbook*. Anyone concerned with secretarial duties and procedures will benefit from the wealth of practical information collected in this convenient pocket edition.

Material has been organized into the key areas of secretarial work, from making telephone and visitor contacts to learning to write correctly. In addition, an introduction, "The Successful Secretary," describes essential personal characteristics and professional techniques, and a Guide to Miscellaneous Data offers more than a dozen pertinent charts and tables. Specific topics can be located easily in the detailed table of contents or the alphabetical index.

The handbook is designed to show you how to do your work better and faster. It is intended to be a day-to-day, practical reference to the multitude of secretarial procedures and practices encountered in nearly every type of business and at each level of professional experience. You cannot help but profit from using it regularly.

The Successful Secretary

The road to success in the secretarial profession is easier to travel when you have the right combination of personal qualities and professional capabilities. The successful secretary always presents a good image to the public, learns what she can about her employer's business, and develops her skills to the highest possible level. Not all secretarial jobs are alike, of course, and the specific combination of ingredients for success will differ from job to job. However, certain personal attributes and professional skills are common to the secretarial profession. The successful secretary has learned what they are.

PERSONAL QUALITIES

The way you look, the way you act, your general attitude and outlook on life, your educational background and job experience, the work habits you develop at the office—all of these things will influence your success in the secretarial field. In measuring their potential, many secretaries think exclusively in terms of experience and job skills, but personal qualities can also tip the scales in a particular direction.

Not everyone will possess all the desirable characteristics mentioned here. But the successful secretary will work daily to improve herself and to come as close as possible to the ideal model. She will develop a pleasing manner and a pleasing voice and will be calm and poised in the presence of others. She will be courteous and show tact and discretion in her daily contacts. Integrity and a sense of ethics are a must in any position, and the successful secretary will become known as a loyal and trustworthy employee. Although she needs to be a good listener, she will try to discourage irresponsible rumors.

Since a negative attitude or outlook on life can be an obstacle to progress, periodic self-evaluation is in order. The successful secretary has a positive outlook. She is helpful and cooperative in dealing with others and is tolerant of clients and co-workers regardless of her personal opinions. As an emotionally mature individual, she is good-natured, objective in disputes, and able to accept criticism and suggestions. She is enthusiastic and has a healthy sense of ambition. She is willing to learn, accept responsibility, and work overtime and generally demonstrates a sincere concern for her employer's business.

Good personal habits are essential. The successful secretary consciously takes steps to stay in good health. Frequent fatigue, poor posture, poor skin tone, and lackluster hair are usually signs that matters of health are being neglected. She also is constantly attentive to cleanliness and personal appearance. Clothing styles and trends keep changing and expectations vary widely from office to office, but as a general rule the successful secretary tends to be conservative in appearance.

Work habits are closely tied to personal traits. For instance, it has become a habit to the successful secretary to be punctual and efficient, to use good diction and good written and spoken English, to be well read and alert, to check and double-check her work for accuracy, to avoid placing or receiving personal calls at work, to be neither abrupt nor long-winded over the telephone, and to avoid clock watching. The successful secretary tries to remember names, to be resourceful in handling assignments, to respect faithfully all confidences, and to avoid discussing business outside the office. She routinely keeps equipment clean, keeps track of supplies (but never takes any home), keeps her desk tidy, sets priorities at work, delegates responsibility among assistants, is attentive to details, and develops her organizational ability to the fullest.

PRINCIPAL DUTIES

One thing can be said with certainty: secretarial work is varied. Even within a particular position duties can be wide ranging. You could be answering the telephone one minute, typing a letter the next, looking for a missing paper in the files after that, then greeting a visitor, and, in between, visiting the neighborhood gift store to do some shopping for your employer. Little wonder that a secretarial career is typically described as interesting and challenging.

Many talents, skills, and general abilities are called forth in a secretarial position. The successful secretary has met the basic qualifications required in all secretarial positions and frequently can offer more. Not surprisingly, the secretary with a broad educational background often finds more opportunities available. A high school education is the minimum requirement, and an additional one- to two-year course in a secretarial school is necessary to qualify for many jobs. These schools offer courses in shorthand, typing, dictation-transcription, and business English. The more education and training, of course, the greater are the chances of a better job and faster promotion. The best jobs and the fastest promotions usually go to those who have received advanced training in junior colleges, vocational and business schools, and colleges and universities. A general education includes courses in the humanities, social sciences, and the sciences. Some specialized jobs, such as legal, scientific, and medical secretarial positions, require appropriate specialized training. In all cases a good command of the English language is vital and, if necessary, a secretary should take courses to improve her written and spoken English.

The successful secretary is an accomplished stenographer and typist. Usually she can take dictation in shorthand or speedwriting at 120 words a minute and transcribe it readily on the typewriter. For straight copy work she can type 70 words a minute and frequently more now that electric typewriters are common. The successful secretary is also familiar with other basic tasks, such as filing, processing mail, and keeping records. A knowledge of business arithmetic, bookkeeping, data processing, and other business subjects can be helpful, too. In general, the successful secretary has a lively interest in the business world, particularly in the field in which her company operates.

The wide scope of secretarial practice becomes obvious when you list the principal tasks performed by secretaries. These include typing; filing; taking and transcribing dictation; meeting people; answering the telephone, placing calls, and screening callers; handling correspondence; processing ingoing and outgoing mail; arranging appointments; keeping books and records; procuring and storing supplies; maintaining expense accounts; arranging travel and meetings; tending to office housekeeping duties; editing and writing; operating office machines; supervising assistants; conducting research; compiling reports; getting material printed; and running the office in the employer's absence. You may not do all of this, but the successful secretary is qualified and prepared to handle many of these things and often more.

Rarely is it enough simply to handle the basic secretarial tasks such as typing and shorthand. There is another critical facet of secretarial procedure: developing effective and efficient techniques. This means not only learning how to type accurately but also learning the many typing shortcuts for centering, feeding envelopes, and so on. The same is true for dictation, record keeping, conducting research, or any other duty. The many timesaving methods described in this handbook can make the difference between progress and status quo in your career.

The successful secretary always does far more than mechanically perform each task. She plans her work load, organizes the work, and schedules it according to priorities; she keeps good records and uses special techniques to file and retrieve material rapidly; she keeps her equipment in good repair and regularly makes use of timesaving machines and desk devices; she uses preprinted forms and other timesaving materials for record-keeping duties; she checks and double-checks everything she writes and types to insure its accuracy; she is careful and thoughtful in her work, never careless or wasteful; and, perhaps above all, she pursues a never-ending program of independent study and self-improvement.

BUSINESS ETIQUETTE

As a secretary, you will be dealing with people both inside and outside your organization. Your success will depend on your approach and your manner. Acceptable behavior and a genuine regard for others are the cornerstones of proper office etiquette, and only when proper etiquette is observed can business be conducted in a cooperative, efficient, and harmonious atmosphere.

The first things a visitor sees are you and your office. For an appropriate personal appearance, good grooming is the key. This means cleanliness; neatness; good posture; dignified, businesslike dress styles; conservative makeup and hair styles; lightly scented perfumes and colognes, if any; and a pleasant, friendly expression. Your hair, makeup, and clothes may require attention during the day, but it is bad manners to attend to grooming at your desk. The office is for business matters. Everything there must be kept clean and tidy at all times—cluttered ashtrays, empty coffee cups, and a trail of crumbs over your desk are unsightly. Depending on your position and the maintenance service your company uses, good housekeeping practices could include some or all of these tasks: daily dusting; cleaning ashtrays, coffee cups, and glasses; sharpening pencils; watering plants; letting in fresh air; and picking up and organizing miscellaneous items.

It is important to learn the basic rules (see chapter 1) for greeting callers, making telephone contacts, and introducing callers. The successful secretary handles all contacts with courtesy, patience, and tact. Moreover, she displays this behavior wherever she goes. In addition, the successful secretary is always punctual for work and appointments.

If the rules of some matters of etiquette are not clear, observe the practice in your office. For example, everyone may appear to be on a first-name basis. But this does not mean you should boldly call the president of your company by his or her first name. Even at parties the informal atmosphere is not an invitation to be overly familiar with others or to behave recklessly.

Money matters can cause problems, and a safe practice is to avoid borrowing and lending. If someone asks, you can always say you are sorry that you did not bring enough with you or that you are taking care of some unexpected bills and have no reserve. Should there be requests for contributions, it is up to you whether you want to give. Also, in an office one usually does not tip either inside or outside service personnel. When traveling with your employer, you should plan on arranging and paying for your own entertainment at night. But the employer customarily pays travel and meal expenses. Secretaries may receive but do not usually buy gifts for their employers. It is a matter of office practice and personal preference whether gifts are exchanged among other co-workers.

Upon the death of an employer or another employee in the same office, a secretary usually sends a letter of condolence (see chapter 9) to the nearest relative and may send flowers as well. Holiday cards are exchanged in some offices. Unfortunately, in some offices what is common practice should not be. Gossip, for instance, may be commonplace, but the successful secretary avoids and discourages it. Also, she absolutely never betrays a personal trust or reveals confidential company matters to anyone, not even to her own family. Neither does she enter into romantic involvements in the office or carry her personal problems to work. Tact comes into play in many situations. It is not necessary, for example, to embarrass someone or hurt someone's feelings. By phrasing a complaint or criticism tactfully and thoughtfully, and presenting it privately, resentment can be avoided. The successful secretary, then, does more than merely learn and follow certain rules; she has a genuine concern for the well-being and the feelings of others.

BUSINESS RELATIONSHIPS

Ideally, relationships are—or should be—a two-way street. In practice, however, the successful secretary learns to work in harmony with others whether or not they meet her halfway. Good human relations are necessary in any office if people are to work together effectively and productively.

The working relationship with an employer is the most important one to a secretary. It will be your responsibility to carry out your employer's instructions. To do this, you must understand your employer's objectives and the problems he or she faces. Although you may offer ideas, it is your job to support your employer's policies and decisions and cooperate fully even when you disagree. However, it is also your duty tactfully to point out obvious errors. In turn, you should willingly accept legitimate suggestions and corrections without becoming defensive. Should your employer be a woman, it is especially important to disregard the myth that women are more difficult to work for than men. Adaptability is often the secret to a successful relationship, particularly when you work for several persons and must adjust to different personalities and expectations. In these circumstances it is important to avoid playing favorites. Sometimes work demands from several executives may conflict, and it may be necessary to explain this to them—tactfully. If the executives are unable to resolve such conflicts, ask the head executive for a decision. In all instances, learn as quickly as possible what is expected of you in terms of skills, initiative, authority, and so forth, and determine immediately what the scope of your job is. The rest will follow.

Often secretaries must work with other departments, clients, and other personnel. Again, adaptability will carry you through—along with a friendly, cooperative attitude. Everyone needs assistance at times, and clients of your firm are paying to receive this help. It pays to develop goodwill both inside and outside your firm. Of course, if someone is taking advantage of your helpfulness, you may have to say no—very politely—or ask your employer for direction when the situation is delicate.

In a secretary-assistant relationship you will be the teacher, supervisor, critic, and manager. Work must be organized and duties delegated to the assistant. Instruction may be necessary. Then the assistant's work must be observed and evaluated. Praise and encouragement should be given when due. Criticism should be constructive and always rendered gently with consideration for the assistant's feelings. A generous supply of appreciation, recognition, and encouragement will produce dividends for the company and create a satisfying, successful relationship for you.

Relationships are between people, and problems are thus inevitable. With your employer you must be supportive and loyal, unless, of course, he or she has a dangerous problem that is threatening your welfare or that of the company. Then you must report it to your employer's immediate superior. You may also discover problems among other personnel, but under no circumstances should a secretary play psychologist or physician. If help is requested, refer the person to an appropriate social agency or qualified professional person. If someone is bothering you with romantic advances, firmly state that you are strongly opposed to getting involved with other personnel. Problems concerning personality clashes can often be overcome by responding with a helpful, thoughtful, and friendly attitude in spite of any personal annoyance with or dislike for the other person. The successful secretary knows that co-workers are not there simply to nourish her own ego. She realizes that, regardless of personal feelings, the prime objective is to develop harmonious working relationships that will benefit her company.

Chapter 1
Making Telephone and Visitor Contacts

The way you communicate with others—
by telephone and in person—directly af-
fects the successful functioning of your office. In fact, the way you handle this task
reflects the image of your entire organization. Whether the caller is a custodian or a
chairman of the board, he or she should be
received promptly and courteously. A secretary must be prepared to handle all
types of visitors in all types of situations.
In addition, she must know how to use the
telephone efficiently and effectively,
screening all incoming calls for her employer. Good judgment is therefore as important as tact and courtesy. Making
telephone and visitor contacts is not only
one of the most common secretarial tasks,
it is one of the most important.

33

RECEIVING CALLERS AT THE OFFICE

When you know in advance that a visitor is coming, you can make appropriate arrangements. But a different approach is needed when the visitor walks in unexpectedly or makes an appointment at the last minute. In all cases the person must be greeted pleasantly, and each visitor's request should be acted on as promptly and thoughtfully as possible, always keeping in mind the employer's needs and wishes.

To receive callers properly at the office, there are several things a secretary must know: (1) how to greet a visitor, (2) how to determine the reason for the visit, (3) how to handle a caller who must wait, (4) procedures to follow if a visitor does or does not have an appointment, (5) how to announce and introduce a visitor to an employer, (6) when and how to refer a caller elsewhere, and (7) how to handle a difficult caller.

Greeting Visitors. Whether you are called to a reception room to escort a visitor to your office or whether the visitor comes directly to your office, your greeting should be cordial but businesslike.

Sometimes the obvious is overlooked: a simple smile and friendly tone of voice go a long way toward making a visitor feel at ease. A pleasant "Good morning" or "How do you do?" will always be well received. But unwarranted familiarity or effusiveness will likely be frowned upon.

If you are seated when a visitor arrives, stop what you are doing and look up immediately. You need not rise unless the visitor is a very prominent individual or an elderly person. Visitors always appreciate being greeted by name, and the efficient secretary makes a strong effort to remember names as well as faces. Of course, if a caller does not have an appointment and you do not recognize the person, you will have to say something such as "May I ask who is calling?" or "May I have your name, please?" Do not make the first move to shake hands, but be prepared in case the visitor offers his or her hand.

When you go into a reception room to meet a caller, be certain to introduce yourself, for example, "Good morning, Mr. Roberts. I'm Mrs. Blackwell's secretary. Will you come with me please?" There is no need to carry on a conversation except for responding politely to the caller's remarks.

Determining the Reason for the Visit. Some callers make it easy by giving their name and stating their business immediately. Others may give their name and merely ask to see your employer. There are several appropriate responses, depending on the situation. You may have to tell the visitor that your employer is out of the office or out of town and ask, "Is there anything I can do for you?" If your employer is busy, you might say, "Mr. Harris isn't free at the moment, but can I be of help?" In these situations most callers reveal the nature of their business by their reply.

When visitors refuse to state the purpose of their call, it is your job to find out what it is. This can be an exasperating exercise. But however frustrating it may be, a secretary should maintain a cool, calm, and cheerful exterior. You may say that you cannot make appointments without knowing what visitors want to discuss: "I'm sorry, Ms. Mason, but Mr. Steinberg has asked me to find out the nature of all calls before scheduling appointments." Make it clear that you do not want details, only a general idea of the matter to be discussed. If that does not work, say you are sorry you cannot help and suggest that the visitor write a confidential letter to your employer.

The Caller Who Must Wait. Visitors may have to wait a few minutes to see your employer, or even longer if they do not have an advance appointment. Either way, offer to hang up a visitor's coat or show the caller where to leave such an item. Then show the visitor where to sit, preferably by a lamp with magazines or other reading matter. But do not ask the caller to wait in your employer's office unless you have prior instructions to that effect. Some visitors may ask to make a telephone call. Point out a private telephone if one is available.

Conversation is not required, although you should respond attentively to any comments the visitor makes. Avoid controversial subjects or discussion of company matters. If you are having a cup of coffee, offer one to the visitor. Otherwise, refreshments are not necessary while a caller is waiting. If you have urgent business to attend to, excuse yourself from the conversation, saying you are rushing to meet a deadline. However, before returning to your work, be certain you have made the visitor comfortable.

Callers with and without Appointments.
The procedure for handling a caller with
an appointment is usually straightforward.
If your organization has a receptionist,
you may want to provide a list of appointments each day so he or she will be prepared for each visitor's arrival. Since your
employer is expecting someone, you can
announce the visitor over the interoffice
communications system as soon as he or
she arrives—unless your employer has
asked not to be interrupted for a few minutes or is away from the office. Then you
should explain the delay and ask the caller
to be seated. At times the unexpected occurs and your employer may be unavoid-
ably delayed a long time. In that case
inform the visitor and offer the option of
waiting or scheduling another appointment.

When a visitor does not have an appointment, you need to consider several
possibilities. The caller may be a very important person, in which case you should
ask your employer right away if he or she
can see the visitor. Sometimes the visitor
is a special friend of your employer, and
you should try to make him or her feel
welcome even though your employer may
be unavailable. When your employer is in
conference and you do not want to inter-

rupt the discussion by using your intercom, take the caller's business card in and quietly hand it to your employer with a typed note asking if he or she will see the visitor. However, if the caller is someone you are sure your employer does not want to see, you will have to discourage making an appointment. You can say your employer will be involved in urgent matters for the foreseeable future and suggest that the visitor write a letter instead.

Announcing and Introducing Visitors. You may announce many of your visitors by intercom. Thus when a visitor has an appointment, you simply buzz your employer and say, "Mr. Lewis is here." Introductions are not needed when the two know each other, so you can then say, "Won't you go right in?" There are times, though, when you might prefer more privacy in announcing someone, to be certain the visitor will not hear your employer's response. In that case you might go into your employer's office and say, "Mrs. McCarthy is outside and would like to talk to you about our inventory. Shall I ask her to come in?" All callers, those with and without appointments, should always be announced immediately—unless you already know that your employer will not see them or you have orders not to interrupt a conference. Some employers prefer that you send in certain persons without announcing them. When you are not sure about your employer's preferences, ask.

When your employer does not know a visitor, an introduction is in order. Make the introduction as the visitor is entering your employer's office. Mention the most important person's name first. If your employer, Mr. Smith, were meeting Mr. Adams, who had a lower ranking position, you would say, "Mr. Smith, this is Mr. Adams." Some executives prefer to come out of their offices to greet each caller personally and introduce themselves.

Referring a Caller Elsewhere. Not everyone knows where to go or whom to see. Some callers must be referred to another person or department. After greeting a visitor and determining the reason for the visit, it should be obvious if the caller is a "misplaced" person. When you know where the visitor should go, explain this carefully and if possible give the caller the name of a person to contact. Be as helpful as possible. You may be able to call another secretary to say that someone is on the way to ask about an appointment.

Someone who is unfamiliar with the people in your organization may be unfamiliar with the physical layout, too. Many visitors, in fact, probably are there for the first time. When they are leaving, it is only common courtesy to point them in the right direction or even escort them to the lobby or elevator if the building is large and the exit difficult to find. If callers overstay their welcome, you may want to remind your employer of the next appointment, thereby also reminding the visitor that it is time to leave. Help the caller collect any personal items and always say good-bye with a smile.

Handling a Difficult Caller. Part of the spice of secretarial life is the difficult caller. Not everyone will accept what you say or take no for an answer. Some people are more than persistent and rude; they are aggressive and unmanageable. Typically the difficult caller is someone who has not made an appointment and insists upon seeing your employer immediately. This person will not accept anything you say and may try to barge right into your employer's office. The caller may be a highly aggressive salesman or a disgruntled employee or someone else with overactive determination.

There are not many courses open to you with a difficult caller. You should, as politely as possible, stick to your guns and insist on the proper procedure for setting up an appointment or refuse to make an appointment if you know that that would be the wish of your employer. If the visitor argues, simply say, "I'm very sorry, but I am not authorized to change our procedures." Suggest that the caller present his or her case in a letter and assure the person that you will make certain that the letter reaches your employer promptly. If a caller becomes threatening, either ring for security if you have it or speak with your employer, privately if possible.

MAKING TELEPHONE CONTACTS

On the surface, making telephone contacts hardly seems to be a mysterious or complicated process. On closer examination, however, the importance of this function to the operations of an organization becomes obvious. The way you handle telephone contacts can build or damage goodwill; it can promote efficiency or create confusion. In short, proper and productive telephone contacts are vital to the welfare of most organizations.

To apply the most effective telephone

techniques, a secretary needs to be thoroughly familiar with (1) the rules of telephone courtesy, (2) how to answer the telephone and transfer calls, (3) how to screen calls, (4) how to place local and long-distance calls, and (5) what to do about problems such as wrong numbers or troublesome callers. (Chapter 3 describes the major types of telephone service, and a map of time zones and area codes is located in the Guide to Miscellaneous Data.)

Telephone Courtesy. It is always a pleasure to speak with someone who sounds friendly, helpful, sincere, and appreciative. But it can be agony to suffer through a conversation with someone who sounds cold, indifferent, annoyed at your intrusion, and generally unfriendly. What you say and how you say it, very simply, creates a good or a bad impression. Courtesy is essential under all circumstances, even when you are saying no to someone. All the rules of proper business etiquette described in the introduction, The Successful Secretary, apply here.

Try to pick up the telephone as soon as it rings and properly identify yourself. Never keep people waiting while you are doing something else. Warn callers if the

wait will be lengthy and offer to call back
in such cases. Always thank callers for
waiting. Have a pencil and paper ready to
take messages or for someone else to use if
you are away from your desk. But never
leave without asking someone to take calls
for you. During conversations listen carefully and do not interrupt the speaker. Be
generous with your thank yous and use
the caller's name while speaking, for example, "Thank you for letting us know,
Mr. Smith." Do not rush the caller but do
not let the conversation go on needlessly,
either. At the end say good-bye pleasantly,
let the caller hang up first, and then gently
replace the receiver.

**Answering the Telephone and Transfer-
ring Calls.** Your office probably has a
standard way of answering the telephone,
such as "Mr. Hall's office." Or "Good
morning, Mr. Hall's office." Or "Good
morning, Mr. Hall's office, Miss Watson
speaking." Or "Mr. Hall's office. May I
help you?" Check with your employer if
you are uncertain. As you answer, speak
with a clear voice and pleasing tone,
enunciating distinctly. Some executives
prefer to take their own calls, which, of
course, will influence what you say when

you answer your own telephone. If you must speak with someone in the office after answering, be sure to cover the mouthpiece.

Transfer calls only when absolutely necessary. If you can handle the call yourself, it is preferable to do so. If you cannot, tell the caller whom it would be best for him or her to speak with. Then ask if the caller wants to be transferred, for instance, "I'm sorry, I don't have that information, Mr. Clark. Ms. Henderson in our Marketing Department takes care of scheduling. I'll be glad to transfer you if you like." If the caller says no, offer to get the necessary information and call back or have the appropriate person call back with the information. Otherwise, stay on the line until you have given the operator the correct name and extension for the transfer. Also, give the caller the extension, in case you are cut off while signaling the operator.

Screening Incoming Calls. The process of screening calls means finding out who is calling and why so you can decide whether your employer would want to speak with the caller. Although many executives prefer to answer their own telephone, you would still be expected to screen calls coming in while your employer is in conference or does not want to be disturbed for some other reason. Some executives want all their calls screened so they do not waste time on matters that could be handled by their secretaries or someone else.

Screening calls is very much like greeting visitors in the office and determining the purpose for their visit. Telephone contacts must also be handled tactfully and courteously, even when a caller refuses to state his or her name and business. (When a caller telephones for an appointment, follow the procedure described in Determining the Reason for the Visit.) Before putting a call through to your employer, say, "May I tell Mr. Sims who is calling?" If your employer also wants you to determine the reason for the call, you might say, "Mr. Sims isn't free at the moment. Could I be of help?" Good judgment is very important in screening calls. Although you should not put through nuisance calls or calls you can clearly handle yourself, neither should you risk offending an important person by refusing to put through a call you are uncertain about. Above all, find out in the beginning your employer's wishes concerning the screening of calls.

Placing Local and Long-Distance Calls.
Just as many executives prefer to answer
their own telephones, they often prefer to
place their own telephone calls. At times,
though, you may have to place the calls
and should follow the proper procedure.
Most calls can be dialed direct, even many
overseas calls (see chapter 3 and also the
map of area codes and time zones in the
Guide to Miscellaneous Data). However,
if the out-of-state party you are calling is
often away, it would be safer to dial Operator and place the call person to person.
Most local telephone numbers will be in
your local directory. Other numbers, local
and out of state, can be obtained by dialing the number for directory assistance.

Let the telephone ring six or seven
times. When someone answers, identify
yourself and ask for the person you are
calling: "This is Ms. Harris from ABC
Company. May I speak with Mr. Arnold,
please?" When you are placing the call for
your employer, say, "Good morning. Is
Mr. Stark there, for Mrs. Anderson of
XYZ Company?" After you are connected, say, "Mr. Stark? Here is Mrs. Anderson," and connect your employer
immediately. Many secretaries connect
their employer as soon as they reach the
other party's secretary. Then, for example,

Mrs. Anderson would be on the line waiting by the time Mr. Stark came on. Follow your employer's wishes for timing.

Handling Problems. Two types of problems are common in telephone contacts: (1) equipment-service problems and dialing errors and (2) troublesome callers. The first type of problem is easily handled. Call your local business office to report any service or equipment problem. Call Operator when the long-distance operator has made a dialing error so you will not be charged for reaching a wrong number. In all cases be courteous to someone you have called in error or someone who has called you in error.

Difficult callers should be handled just as you would handle a troublesome visitor in your office. (See Handling a Difficult Caller, page 41.) For instance, politely recommend that they write a confidential letter if they want an appointment but refuse to give their name or state their business. Crank or obscene calls should be reported immediately to your local telephone company.

Chapter 2
Handling Incoming and Outgoing Mail

The volume may vary from day to day, but one thing you can always expect is the mail. In fact, in some offices there is more than one mail delivery. In small companies the mailman will probably deliver the mail directly to you; in large organizations a company mail clerk or messenger may distribute it to each department or office. Either way, most executives are eager to receive important communications, and it is the secretary's responsibility to process incoming mail quickly and efficiently. Since important communications go out as well as come in each day, it is also the secretary's duty to see that outgoing mail is prepared properly and sent without delay. To handle this important daily function, you need to have a good understanding of two things: efficient procedures and current postal regulations.

HOW TO PROCESS INCOMING MAIL

One speaks of "processing" incoming mail because several things must be done to it as soon as it arrives. How you handle incoming mail is important to everyone. Not only will efficient procedures avoid a chaotic accumulation of paperwork in the office, but they will also relieve your employer of time-consuming attention to details.

To process the incoming mail quickly and carefully, you need to know (1) how to open and sort mail, (2) how to prepare mail for your employer and route the other material, (3) how to handle mail when your employer is away, and (4) how to treat different categories of mail—newspapers, letters, bills, and so forth.

Opening and Sorting the Mail. Before you open the mail, sort it into major categories. What categories to use depends on the type of work in your office. For instance, invoices might be a major category in one office but not in another. Five common categories of mail are (1) personal and confidential letters; (2) telegrams, letters, and other business correspondence;

(3) invoices; (4) advertisements, circulars, and miscellaneous packages; and (5) newspapers, books, and periodicals. With time you will learn which items are of greatest interest to your employer. Most executives want to see urgent material, such as a telegram or special delivery letter, as quickly as possible. If your mail volume is heavy at times, consider using racks, trays, or some of the other sorting aids sold in stationery and office supply stores.

Once you have organized the unopened mail into stacks for each major category, open items in the most important categories first. However, you should never open a letter marked "Personal" or "Confidential." The stack of telegrams, letters, and other business correspondence will probably be number one on your priority list. Tap the bottom edge of each envelope so you do not mutilate the contents when you slit open the flaps or shave off the tops with an electric opener. After opening the mail, remove all contents carefully and attach any enclosures to the letters with paper clips. Check if anything is missing. Do not destroy an envelope when there is no address on the enclosed letter. Also, if the letter is not dated, mark the postmark date on it before discarding the envelope. Some offices rubber-stamp all mail with the date received.

There are ways to speed the opening process. For example, stack the envelopes face down with the flaps on the same side so you can slit all of them open in rapid succession. Hand-operated and electric machines will speed the stacking and opening process even more. Check addresses as you are organizing the mail, before opening it, to avoid opening someone else's mail in error. Packages need to be cut with a knife or scissors. Before discarding the wrapping, always check to see if a letter is taped to the outside. Also, you may need to salvage the address label if the contents do not include the sender's address. Interoffice mail usually comes in unsealed envelopes that are used over and over, so no cutting or slitting is needed.

Preparing and Routing the Mail. After the mail is opened, you sort again. This time, with the contents fully visible, you can divide everything into mail for your own attention, mail intended for your employer, and mail to be routed to other persons. The first order of business is to prepare your employer's mail. Next you should get ready the material to be routed, and last take care of the mail meant for your own attention.

How you prepare your employer's mail depends on the practice in your office and your employer's wishes. But certain steps are common in most offices. Unless you scan the mail, you will not know what to do. Some letters, for instance, will raise issues about which your employer will need information. If time permits, collect and attach helpful background information to the correspondence before presenting it to your employer. Otherwise make a note to look for the information while your employer is reading the mail. Often a letter will refer to previous correspondence that you can quickly pull from the files. Be prepared to annotate mail if your employer requests it. This is often done by underlining key words and phrases with a yellow marking pen (which does not show if a document is photocopied) and making notes in the margins to help answer any questions the sender poses. Check facts and figures in the letter for accuracy. If a handwritten letter is hard to read, type a copy of it and attach it to the original. Just before you give the mail to your employer, arrange it with the most important items on top. Also, segregate newspapers and other reading material from correspondence and priority business matters. Personal letters, too, should be kept apart from the business mail.

Preprinted routing slips save time when you must forward mail to someone else. Some mail is simply missent, as the outside address clearly shows. Other mail, though addressed to your office, may concern a matter best handled by someone else. Find out if your employer wants to see such mail before you forward it. Staple a printed slip to the mail being routed and send it out with your other interoffice mail. These slips usually have a space at the top for the date and the name of the person to whom it should be sent. Beneath that there is a preprinted list where you can check off any instructions you have, for example, please handle, please note and return, or please note and forward to the appropriate person. Always handle mail to be routed out of your office as carefully and efficiently as you would your own material.

When Your Employer Is Away. Some secretaries keep a daily register of all incoming mail and a record of all outgoing mail. Mimeographed forms or pages with columns in a loose-leaf notebook are appropriate for such logs. Even though your office may not require this type of daily record, it is helpful to have it when your employer is traveling. Having such summaries in front of you makes it easy to report on daily mail activity when your employer telephones the office. Also, many executives like to receive copies of such records while they are traveling as a quick means of learning what is happening at the office. How much information you summarize will depend on what your employer wants to know. Usually an incoming mail record shows type of mail, date received, date sent, sender, and action taken (or to be taken). An outgoing mail record typically summarizes date sent, description (of the communication sent), addressee, action requested, and follow-up date. (A digest of this type could easily be expanded to include telephone calls and office visits as well as mail activity.)

In addition to keeping mail records to send your employer and to refer to when he or she telephones, have the mail sorted and ready for quick reference while you are on the phone. When there is something urgent in the mail, do not wait for a call, however. Send a telegram or telephone your employer's hotel right away. Acknowledge all correspondence (see chapter 9), explaining your employer's absence and expected return date, or refer correspondence to others for reply. Of course, you should handle whatever you can yourself. If your employer wants to receive important letters and reports while traveling, send photocopies but not the originals. It helps to number packets you forward so your employer can watch to be sure they all arrive safely. The mail that you keep in the office for your employer's return should be organized by category, with letters placed in file folders, for example, priority correspondence requiring attention; correspondence for your information and review; reports; advertisements and miscellaneous circulars; and books, newspapers, and periodicals.

How to Treat Different Classes of Mail. It is surprising how often different categories of incoming mail are treated incorrectly. Good judgment is an important quality for secretaries who must handle the mail each day. The first requirement is to realize that communications do not always specify their relative importance. A letter of request, for example, may ask for information to use at a meeting scheduled in exactly one week. The letter may appear routine and insignificant, particularly if it does not use words such as *urgent* or *rush.* But this request clearly needs immediate attention because of the meeting date. On the other hand, an advertisement may have the words *URGENT* or *RUSH* printed in bold letters across the envelope, but this is probably an advertising tactic. Mail that concerns important business matters or that involves a deadline for someone must be treated expeditiously. However, the judgment about which communications are truly urgent and which are not is yours to make.

Another incorrect assumption made in business offices concerns advertising material. Some secretaries automatically toss anything that looks like an ad (so-called junk mail) in the wastebasket without opening it. It is a mistake to treat this class of mail so casually. Many of these letters contain important announcements of new products that would keep your employer aware of competition and technological advancements, of new books that your employer should read to stay up to date in his or her field, and of seminars or conferences that your employer might want to attend. Again, good judgment is needed so you do not overload your employer with nonessential literature, but neither should you routinely assume everything in this category of mail is useless.

HOW TO PREPARE OUTGOING MAIL

Whether or not your organization has a mail room, there are a number of things you need to know about handling the outgoing mail. It is up to the secretary in an office to see that addresses are correct, that all letters are signed, that no enclosures are forgotten, and so forth. Then there are decisions to be made about the class of mail and any special services to use. Should something be sent special delivery? Does it need registering and, if so, at what value? As you can see, the process of preparing material for mailing involves a great deal more than licking postage stamps.

To handle the preparation of outgoing mail accurately and efficiently, you need to know (1) how to use effective mailing techniques and equipment; (2) how to get and check signatures on outgoing mail; (3) how to assemble, fold, and insert letters and other material; and (4) how to handle enclosures.

Using Effective Mailing Techniques. An efficient secretary checks and double-checks her work. The best way to insure that outgoing mail is prepared properly and accurately is to double-check letter and envelope addresses, signatures on the letters, the enclosures, carbon-copy notations, special mailing notations, and anything else that determines where something is going, to whom, and by what class or service of mail. If this task is new to you, type a checklist to follow each time you prepare the mail until it becomes second nature to verify each item before sealing and mailing the communications.

Check carefully for errors and omissions. For instance, the inside address and the address on the envelope or mailing label must match. Each should have a complete name, street, city, two-letter state abbreviation (see the list in the Guide to Miscellaneous Data), and zip code. (When nine-digit zip codes are available, use them to facilitate rapid mail delivery.) All correspondence should be signed, of course, and envelopes prepared for carbon copies directed to others. Enclosures should be double-checked against each letter. (See also Assembling the Mail and Handling Enclosures, page 62.) Mailing notations such as *Special Delivery* or *Confidential* must be typed or rubber-stamped on each envelope (see chapter 9). Watch for postscripts or corrections your employer adds to outgoing letters and make the same changes on the carbon copies. Set aside letters to be retyped.

Once you have double-checked, assembled, and inserted everything, organize your letters and packages in the most efficient manner. Segregate mail requiring special handling. In fact, separate each class of mail (e.g., first class, third class, and so on) and within a class sort it into local, out-of-town, and out-of-state delivery. Mail rooms often presort mail by zip code to expedite handling by the Postal Service. For current regulations concerning each class of mail, consult your local post office (see also Important Postal Information, page 65). Depending on your mail volume, you may have a postage meter to use, which will greatly speed the stamping and sealing steps.

Getting Signatures on Outgoing Mail. You would think that something as obvious as signing a letter does not warrant much attention. But almost everyone at some time has received an unsigned letter. It is amazing how easily such oversights occur when secretaries do not make it a point always to double-check the signature on each communication. The most obvious thing to look for is whether the signature is on the letter. But there is more. Did you type J. A. Parker and did your employer sign it Jack Parker (see chapter 9)? If you signed the letter for your employer, did you remember to initial it? It is important to keep in mind that unsigned or improperly signed documents are invalid. So this kind of oversight or error can be more serious than most people realize.

The likelihood of something going out unsigned can be reduced if you follow a certain procedure each time you prepare correspondence. First separate the typed letters into categories that will be obvious to your employer. Urgent correspondence should always be placed on top. In addition, you might separate letters your employer dictated from those you composed on your own for his or her signature. Keep the carbon copies on your desk until the originals have been mailed. Should your employer change an original, you would then have the carbon copy handy to make the same change on it *before* you put it in the files.

Depending on the practice in your office, you will present the letters for signature either with or without the envelopes attached. If your employer does not want to be bothered with the envelopes, you can submit the letters and type the envelope addresses from the carbon copies while the originals are being signed. Otherwise, follow this procedure: (1) remove the carbon copies and clip enclosures back of the letter in the left corner, and (2) place the envelope flap over the letter and enclosures. After you pick up the letters from your employer, examine each signature and check the enclosures to see that everything is signed and still in proper order before you fold and insert the material.

Assembling the Mail and Handling Enclosures. By the time you are ready to dispatch the mail, you should have all enclosures in proper order. You also should have checked whether covering letters have proper enclosure notations (see chapter 9). The enclosures may be stapled together if necessary, but the U.S. Postal Service discourages the use of paper clips, which can tear envelopes and damage postal machines. Although most enclosures are *not* stapled to the letters, there is one exception to this practice. Very small enclosures such as business cards and tiny pieces of paper are sometimes stapled to the front, upper left corner of a letter, with the smallest item on top. Otherwise small enclosures are tucked inside the last fold of a letter.

Small enclosures (smaller than the covering letter) are often placed inside the last fold of a letter so the recipient will be certain to pull out everything at once from the envelope. But large enclosures (larger than the covering letter) will have to be folded so the letter fits inside them. Of course, if the enclosures are much larger than the letter, everything may have to be mailed flat in an appropriate-sized manila envelope. Other possibilities are to mail the letter and enclosures separately (the letter by first-class mail and the enclosures by third-class mail) or to attach the covering letter in an envelope (with first-class postage) to the outside of the larger manila envelope (containing third-class postage).

Enclosures come in all types and sizes. With odd-sized items the standard methods of handling described above may be inappropriate. For example, coins and stamps could easily be lost if placed loose within the fold of a letter. Yet a coin cannot be stapled to a letter. The two most common procedures used with such objects are (1) to place them in small cellophane envelopes or (2) if it will not damage the items, to tape them to a card, which is then stapled to the covering letter or slipped inside the last fold of the letter.

Folding and Inserting the Mail. A neatly folded letter makes a good impression on the receiver. Follow this procedure when you fold an 8½- by 11-inch letter for insertion into a long (no. 10) envelope (or a monarch letter into a monarch envelope): Fold the letter once slightly less than one-third of the way up from the bottom. Then make a final fold so there is one-eighth to one-fourth inch of the letter still showing at the top edge. For an 8½- by 11-inch letter going into a smaller (no. 6¾) envelope, fold the letter almost in half, again leaving one-eighth to one-fourth inch at the top. Then fold from the right to the left slightly less than one-third of the way over. Make the last fold from the left to the right, this time leaving one-eighth to one-fourth inch of the letter showing at the right edge. Some secretaries find that it helps to judge the various measurements by first placing the letter flat under the flap of the envelope, using the bottom edge of the envelope as a guide to making the first fold.

How you insert letters or other material depends on the type and size material and the type of envelope. When you use a window envelope, for example, the item being inserted must be placed so all of the address shows clearly through the window opening. In most cases letters are inserted into envelopes with the one-eighth- to one-fourth-inch margin showing when the envelope is opened. The recipient will then be able to pull out the letter, open it, and unfold it with the type side up and ready for reading. Folding and inserting one letter according to the steps described here may seem simple, and it is. With time, in fact, it will become almost automatic. But there are frequently a number of items to mail, and to save time, you need to streamline the entire operation. For instance, it speeds the inserting process to arrange all envelopes in succession with flaps open. Handling enclosures with one hand and envelopes with the other, you can insert enclosures in rapid sequence from the top to the bottom envelope. Take special care when you do this, however, to keep enclosures and envelopes in the correct order or you will have letters going in the wrong envelopes to the wrong places.

IMPORTANT POSTAL INFORMATION

After a communication is addressed, assembled, and inserted, you are ready for the final steps in handling outgoing mail. To complete your work efficiently and economically, you must have certain basic information about current postal regulations. Since rates and other aspects of postal service keep changing with time, it pays to contact your local postmaster periodically for up-to-date information. In addition, postal personnel will advise you about available mailing equipment and time- and money-saving methods of preparing all classes of mail. For further details you can also request free copies of available pamphlets and rate sheets, or you may purchase chapters 1 to 6 of the *Postal Manual* (ask about current subscription prices and cost of the loose-leaf supplementary service). The following sections highlight the major domestic and international postal services and regulations. (For a list of the official two-letter state abbreviations approved by the U.S. Postal Service, consult the Guide to Miscellaneous Data.)

Domestic Postal Service. Although some offices handle a heavy volume of foreign correspondence, most secretaries are especially concerned with domestic mailings. As postage and labor costs continue to rise, organizations become more and more concerned with efficiency and economy measures. Secretaries who handle some or many aspects of communications are expected to develop sound time- and cost-saving techniques and to keep abreast of changing postal rates and regulations. Contact your local post office for current rates, special fees, and size and weight limitations applicable to each class of mail or special service described below.

First-class (and priority) mail is the fastest class of domestic mail. It is also more expensive than second-, third-, or fourth-class mail. First-class mail is automatically sent by air service (when practical) without additional postage. When a first-class item weighs between 13 ounces and 70 pounds, it is designated *priority mail.* First-class and priority articles may be sealed against postal inspection.

Second-class mail service is usually selected for the bulk mailing of newspapers and periodicals. The publications must be published at least four times a year and must bear the printed notice of second-class entry. Publishers may add civic or public-service messages to wrappers or covers provided the messages are free, not paid advertisements. The general public may also mail a newspaper or periodical at this class by writing *Second-Class Matter* above the address.

Third-class mail is often used for circulars, books and catalogs over 24 pages, and a variety of merchandise—with a 16-ounce weight limit. Although this mail may be sealed, it is subject to postal inspection. Packages should be clearly marked, for example, *Printed Matter* or *Merchandise.* Organizations that want to mail large quantities of items at this rate may purchase a bulk mailing permit and, by following regulations for sorting and delivery, mail at the bulk third-class rate. Even lower nonprofit rates are available to organizations that qualify.

Fourth-class mail applies to printed matter and merchandise over 16 ounces. This class is used for mailing parcels, books, recordings, and so forth, at an economical rate. Parcel post postage is determined by delivery zone. A special fourth-class rate is available for books over 24 pages, certain films, and library materials. Bulk mailings may be made by fourth-class mail, with postage indicated by permit imprint. All fourth-class matter is subject to postal inspection. Your local post office can advise you about the many restrictions pertinent to this class of domestic service.

Business-reply mail is used when you want an envelope or card to come back to you. Mailers pay an annual fee and agree to pay a nominal amount for each item that comes back. Return cards or envelopes must show a permit imprint and return address. Also, the words *BUSINESS REPLY MAIL* must be prominently displayed, along with the notice "Postage will be paid by . . ." or "No postage stamp necessary if mailed in the United States."

Express mail guarantees rapid delivery of your mail to most cities in the United States, for example, next-day service, same-day airport service, or custom-designed service (such as door-to-door). Almost any type of item may be mailed with this high-speed service, but it is especially useful for urgent messages and time-sensitive products.

Private messenger and transfer services are also available for rapid delivery of mail. Companies providing such services are listed in the Yellow Pages of the telephone directory.

Mailgram is another fast service. Messages are telephoned or delivered to a local Western Union office. From there they are immediately transmitted by wire to a post office near the destination for postal delivery the same or the following business day. A similar service, ECOM (electronic computer-originated mail), is being designed to provide two-day delivery service.

Special delivery is available at most post offices. Important letters and packages and perishable items will be delivered immediately upon reaching the post office at the destination.

Special handling is used for perishable items or important material that you want transported expeditiously. But this service is available only for third- and fourth-class mail, and it does not provide for special delivery at the destination.

Certified mail is used when you want to be certain an item (with no real money value) has reached someone. A mailing receipt and record of delivery are returned to you after the recipient accepts the article.

Certificates of mailing give you a record to prove something was mailed. But a certificate does not provide a record that anyone received the article. Forms to complete are available from your local post office.

Registered mail allows for insurance coverage for first-class or priority mail, properly sealed, up to a liability of $10,000. You must declare the value of the item being mailed at the time you pay the registry fee. This service is especially useful for valuable material such as deeds or stock certificates.

Return receipts may be purchased for both registered and certified mail and for certain insured parcels. These receipts give you signed proof that an item was delivered.

Insured mail applies to third- and fourth-class mail (first-class and priority mail must be registered to qualify for insurance coverage). The fee depends on the value of the item. Packages must be securely wrapped according to regulations for the class of mail being used.

C.O.D., or collect-on-delivery, service may be used when the recipient has agreed in advance to pay for the merchandise upon receipt. C.O.D. service may be used for merchandise sent by parcel post, third-class mail, or first-class mail.

Money orders, used in lieu of checks or bank drafts, may be purchased and cashed at any post office. Proper identification is required to redeem a postal money order.

Mailing aids, to make your job easier and speed up mail delivery, are available from the U.S. Postal Service and commercial establishments such as office supply stores. Some things you should be familiar with are postage meter machines; precanceled stamps; printed permit imprints; mail sorting devices; the zip code directory; labels, mailing envelopes, and parcel preparation supplies; and self-inking stampers. In addition, the Postal Service urges mailers to follow certain practices: (1) mail early in the day, (2) always use zip codes and presort mail by zip code and class of mail, (3) use the right postage and use metered mail rather than stamps if possible, (4) use the recommended two-letter state postal abbreviations (see Guide to Miscellaneous Data), (5) have packages clearly marked for special services such as certified mail, and (6) prepare envelopes and packages precisely according to regulations for each class of mail.

International Postal Service. Regulations and fees for mail to other countries are completely different from domestic fees and restrictions. Moreover, they differ widely from country to country. Ask for a free copy of Publication 51 from your local post office or purchase a *Directory of International Mail* (contact the Superintendent of Documents, U.S. Government Printing Office, Washington, D.C. 20402).

Letters and letter packages represent a major class of international mail. Included in this category are ordinary letters, packages with letters, and typewritten material. You should write *Letter* on any item that might be mistaken for another type of parcel. Always mark *Par Avion* on articles to go by air service. Forms must be completed for merchandise subject to customs duty.

Printed matter refers to newspapers, periodicals, books, pamphlets, greeting cards, sheet music, catalogs, drawings, unframed photographs, calendars, maps, advertisements, printed reproductions of handwriting or typewriting, and so on. Leave packages unsealed, write *Printed Matter* on the wrapper, and specify the nature of the contents, for example, *Books.*

Postcards may be sent by surface on air. Rates for postcards are uniform from country to country, except for Canada and Mexico. Only single cards are allowed, and there are minimum and maximum allowable dimensions, depending on the country. However, business reply cards (and envelopes) are prohibited.

Small packets are items of merchandise and samples that do not weigh more than 2 pounds 3 ounces. *Small Packet* should be written on the wrapper, and the package should be left unsealed. *Sample* or *Gift* should be written on the outside of packages not intended for sale. Eight-ounce merchandise packets can be sent without a customs declaration.

Commercial papers are originals and copies of documents that may be written or drawn but are not considered personal correspondence. Examples are invoices, literary manuscripts, and insurance policies. Packages must be unsealed and *Commercial Papers* must be written on the outside.

Aerogrammes are sheets of stationery that can be folded and sealed for mailing alone without an extra envelope. No enclosures are permitted. These communications typically have postage and airmail notations preprinted on them. The rate for aerogrammes is uniform from country to country.

Parcel post packages may be sent by surface vessel or air service to almost any country in the world. But size and other restrictions vary from country to country, and customs regulations differ as well. A special handling service is available from local U.S. post offices to the International Exchange office.

Special services are available for international as well as domestic mail. For example, parcel post registration, insurance, and special delivery are available to certain countries. Secretaries who want to enclose return postage may purchase international reply coupons, which the recipient can exchange for postage.

Chapter 3
Using Telephone and Telegraph Services

Numerous contacts in the business world are made by telephone and telegraph. In some offices, in fact, telephone and wire messages make up the major portion of internal and external communications. The secretary who has a good understanding of available services and how to use them properly is an asset to her employer. The first thing a secretary should do is become familiar with the telephone and wire services and the equipment used in her own office. Of course, to select the most efficient, effective, and economical means of communication, you must be aware of the advantages and disadvantages of all of the major types of service and equipment and keep abreast of the latest developments.

MAJOR TELEPHONE SERVICES

In addition to the personal aspects of telephone communications (described in chapter 1), you need to know something about the technical and mechanical aspects. Telephone contacts are indispensable in today's fast-paced, competitive business world, and the right telephone service and equipment are essential for successful operations. Just as important as selecting the best service and equipment, however, is the ability to use what you have effectively and productively. Improper use can result in lost sales, a damaged image, and wasted time and expense. The wise secretary learns as much as she can as soon as she can about the different services and how to use them. This includes (1) station-to-station and person-to-person calls; (2) international direct-distance dialing (IDDD); (3) mobile and marine calls; (4) conference, appointment, and messenger calls; (5) equipment and convenience aids; and (6) special services for business.

Station-to-Station and Person-to-Person Calls. When you call out of town, two options are open to you. You can dial direct, at a lower rate, and speak with anyone who answers, or you can dial the operator for assistance and have the call placed to a specific person, at a higher rate. On any out-of-town call, of course, rates also vary according to how long you talk, the distance involved, and the time of day. Your local telephone business office and your local directory will give you full details on rates, procedures for securing operator assistance and information, direct-dialing procedures, and so forth.

A *station-to-station call* is made by dialing the correct area code and telephone number (see map of time zones and area codes in the Guide to Miscellaneous Data). From some locations you also must first dial an access number such as 1. (Should you reach a wrong number, hang up and immediately dial the operator. Give her the incorrect state you reached, to avoid being charged for the call.) With a station-to-station call you must speak with anyone at the number called, and charges begin the moment someone answers. If this will not cause an undesirable delay, or if you need not speak with a particular person, the lower cost station-to-station call may be the best choice.

A *person-to-person call* is made by dialing the operator (dial 0) and giving the name of the person you want to speak with as well as the person's number. The operator will then ask for your telephone number for billing purposes. With this type of call, charges do not begin until the designated person comes on the line. The question is whether you want to pay the higher rate for a person-to-person call and be assured that you will not pay for any time until the person you want comes on the line and that you will not be charged at all if the designated person is not there.

International Direct-Distance Dialing (IDDD). From many locations you can now dial direct to 18 other countries, such as Italy, Australia, and Japan. Without IDDD you would have to dial the operator and give the name of the person you are calling, the country, and the telephone number. (Because of the cost involved, your employer might also expect you to ask the operator to give you time and charges on the call for your records.) Using IDDD, you would simply dial the international access code, the country code, the city code, and then the local telephone number. Of course, you must speak with anyone who answers when you dial direct, just as you would do when dialing direct within the United States.

Mobile and Marine Calls. You can call to and from almost any location nowadays, including a moving motor vehicle or a ship, if the receiver has the proper equipment for telephone communications. Equipment installed in a vehicle such as a car or truck is called a *mobile telephone.* Numbers for such units are listed in the telephone directory just as they are for other resident and business telephones. The telephone itself can be installed anywhere in the vehicle that is convenient, although the transmitter-receiver unit is usually positioned out of sight, for example, in the trunk. Conveniences such as an answering service may be used with a mobile telephone as well as with a stationery unit. Mobile calls are placed and received in the same way that they are with a regular telephone.

Marine calls refer to communications sent to and from a boat or ship at sea. When a ship has the proper equipment and is within calling range, you can reach someone by first dialing the operator. Next you would ask to speak with the marine operator. Give this operator the ship's name, the name of the person you want to reach, the cabin or stateroom number if you know it, and the telephone number if there is one. (Your employer may expect you to ask the operator to give you time and charges for your records.) Some ships also use a direct line hookup while they are in the harbor. This allows callers to dial direct when the ship is docked. Keep in mind that mobile and marine calls, like any other call, are both subject to rate variations, time differences, and so on. Consult your directory and local telephone company for current rates and regulations.

Conference, Appointment, and Messenger Calls. You can make special arrangements with the operator to call someone at a set time or to speak with several persons in different locations all at the same time or to send a message to someone who has no telephone. If your employer wants to make a *conference call,* for example, you start by dialing the operator and asking for the conference operator. This operator will need to know the names and telephone numbers of everyone who will participate in the telephone conference and the time desired for the arrangement. When time permits, the operator will contact each person in advance to confirm the time. Once the appointments are set, the operator will reserve any necessary conference equipment and follow through at the designated time. Each connection is charged as if it were an individual person-to-person call.

The time reservation described above is also sometimes referred to as an *appointment call*. When you place any long-distance, person-to-person call, you may give the operator a specific time that you want to speak with someone. The operator will then attempt to make your connection at the requested time. Appointment calls may be necessary when your employer or the person being called has a hectic schedule. Some situations are complicated further when the person you are calling is not near a telephone. A *messenger call* might solve this problem. Ask the operator at the destination to send a messenger for the person you are calling. Charges include the cost of messenger service plus the usual cost of a person-to-person call.

Equipment and Convenience Aids. If you watch advertisements or visit telephone company display rooms, you will be aware of the wide variety of equipment styles, supplementary devices, and miscellaneous convenience aids to choose from. The designer's touch is evident in color selections, with standard and decorator colors to fit any decor. But the real question is what these things can do for you and your organization. The complexity of the equipment and devices in your office will depend on the size of your organization and its particular needs. Although a standard telephone with a hold button and a buzzer may suffice in a small office, a larger facility will likely have switchboard equipment, loudspeaker equipment, automatic dialing telephones, sophisticated signaling devices, and so on. A representative from your local telephone company can bring you up to date on the latest models and special features of interest to you.

The three most common *switching systems* are the PBX (private branch exchange) switchboards, the telephone console (a cordless, desk-top switchboard), and, for large-volume users, the Centrex system (direct dialing to office extensions). Telephone equipment keeps changing with advances in technology, and something new is always appearing on the market. But some things, like the switching systems, are apt to be around for a while. For example, the *Speakerphone,* a telephone with microphone and loudspeaker, is now available in a compact model that allows no-hands-needed conversations anywhere in the office or even at home in the kitchen. *Automatic dialing telephones* store numbers on cards or tape. You need only push a button or insert a plastic card in a slot and the number is automatically dialed for you. Telephone companies also have a variety of miscellaneous devices to make your job easier. For instance, you can get a *plug-in headset* that will let you listen to dictation over the telephone, leaving both hands free to type.

The Telephone Directory. One of the most useful reference tools in the business world is the telephone directory. Even so, many persons fail to take advantage of the wealth of information it offers. In addition to providing alphabetical listings of persons and organizations, the directory's Yellow Pages are invaluable when you are searching for information about some product or service. Directories for other cities may be purchased by calling your local telephone company business office and requesting that the order be charged to your telephone. Some secretaries supplement their telephone directory with a desk telephone book or list. Here they record—and periodically update—frequently called numbers, for example, company business numbers (airlines, messenger services, telegraph office, and so on) and personal numbers (doctors, travel agencies, florists, and so on).

Special Services for Business. People who are away from their homes or offices find that calling long distance is simplified when they have a *credit card.* Telephone companies will issue a credit card free of charge upon request. The card is good for use anywhere in the United States and Canada and from Bermuda and the Caribbean Islands to the United States. In addition, more than one hundred countries protected by Teleplan accept credit card calls back to the United States.

In some situations telephones would be unattended if it were not for the use of an *answering service.* Independent answering services arrange for a connection to your telephone and provide trained operators to cover your calls—answer them, take messages, and so on. Automatic answering systems activate prerecorded messages and then tape incoming messages for later playback.

WATS (Wide-Area Telephone Service) is one of the common business services for companies that make a lot of long-distance calls. An access line is connected to a dialing network that covers a state, a region, or the entire nation. Using two machines, *Data-Phone* service lets you convert and transmit any type of information (photograph, map, and so on) over the regular telephone lines. *Teletypewriter* service provides rapid communication between two or more points. (Teletypewriters are also used in conjunction with Data-Phone service.) *Picturephone* lets you see callers, documents, and so forth. *Tie lines* connect two offices directly, for example, a headquarters office and a branch office.

PRINCIPAL TELEGRAPH SERVICES

When you need a written record of your message but do not have time to correspond by letter, the telegram is a logical choice. Secretaries often have to do more than type a message. You may be expected to decide which class of telegraph service to use; to write the message, or rewrite it to reduce its size and thus its cost; and to send the message to a local Western Union office after typing it. Since speed is so important, a secretary should know in advance how to use both domestic and international services.

Domestic Service. The three principal classes of domestic service are the fast telegram, the night letter, and the mailgram. Which service you select depends on how much time you have and how much you want to spend. When speed is the most important consideration, you may decide on the *fast telegram.* There is a minimum rate for 15 words and an additional charge for every word thereafter. These messages are often delivered within a couple of hours. The *night letter* is less expensive. Charges are for a minimum of 100 words and a small fee for each group of 5 words thereafter. Messages may be sent until midnight, and delivery is usually made the following morning. *Mailgrams* are wired to a post office at the destination for delivery in the next regular mail. A message of up to 100 words may be sent at standard Western Union rates plus a special delivery charge.

There are other types of telegraph services, many of them involving new, automated communications equipment and systems. A few of the more common systems are Telex, TWX, and Datagram. *Telex* Teletypewriters can rapidly send messages worldwide, manually or automatically, at low cost. *TWX* is a similar but slightly faster manual or automatic transmission service. Telex and TWX users can also communicate with each other by means of a computer interface. *Data-gram* receives and converts messages into a teletypewritten record, which is then transmitted by Telex or TWX. One of the fastest ways to send money is by telegraph. *Money orders* are easily transmitted by wire to any point in the United States and to most other countries as well.

International Service. Like domestic messages, international telegrams, or cablegrams, can also be sent through your local Western Union office. Or you can file them directly with one of the international carriers such as ITT, RCA, WUI (Western Union International), or French Cable. Since each carrier serves different overseas cities, you may want to check the routes for each.

The two main classes of cablegrams are the full-rate message and the letter telegram. *Full-rate messages (FR)* are the quickest type of cablegram. Distance determines the charge per word, with a minimum charge for 7 words. Code messages *must* be sent FR. *Cable letters (LT)* are less expensive—about half of the FR cost per word, with a 22-word minimum. This is an overnight service, appropriate for longer messages that can wait until the following day for delivery.

For *radio shore-to-ship* messages indicate the name of the ship, the passenger's name, the cabin or stateroom number (if known), and the coastal radio station through which the ship can be reached (e.g., Newyorkradio). *Radio photo service* lets you send photographs, drawings, typewritten material, contracts, and so forth, by radio transmission. *Overseas Telex* service gives you a teleprinter connection to more than 150 countries. Some arrangements, such as *leased channel,* offer economical service to large-volume users. To cut the usual cost of charges for both addresses and signatures, you can use a *registered code address.* Check with one of the international carriers, a local Western Union office, or a nearby central bureau of registered addresses for information on securing a registered code address.

How to Count Charges. Western Union has a chart that shows you how to count *charges for domestic telegrams.* The following rules apply: (1) Essential material in one full address is free, but there is a charge for additional or alternate names and addresses. (2) The sender's name and company name are free, but there is a charge for the sender's street address, department, and title (if used). The sender's city and state appear (free) in the dateline. (3) Punctuation marks are free, but charges are made for words such as *stop*. (4) Dictionary words up to and including 15 characters count as one word each. Combinations of words, not forming a dictionary word, are counted as one word per 5 letters or fraction thereof. (5) Proper names and personal names are counted according to the way they are usually written. Miami Beach is thus two words, even if written as Miamibeach. (6) Initials such as J.C. are counted as one word without a space. But J. C. with a space would be two words. (7) Groups of letters and figures, including signs such as $, are counted at the rate of one word for each 5 characters (e.g., $17.95 = one word), except to Canada, Saint Pierre, and the Miquelon Islands. To those places each individual figure or sign is counted as a separate word.

One of the international carriers will give you a chart explaining how to count *charges for cables*. The rules differ from those for domestic telegrams: (1) In the address everything is counted at 15 letters or fraction thereof per word, except the place of destination is counted as one word in spite of length. Names and streets can be run together and counted as one word per 15 letters or fraction thereof (e.g., Lemondestreet = one word). (2) Signatures are also counted at 15 letters or fraction thereof per word. (3) Throughout the text each dictionary word of 15 letters or less equals one word. A word containing 20 letters, for example, would be counted as two words. (4) In code, 5 characters or fraction thereof are counted as one word. Remember, though, that messages with code must always be sent FR. (5) Groups of figures and signs are counted at the rate of 5 characters or fraction thereof per word. But some symbols such as $ must be spelled out. (6) Abbreviations such as C.O.D. are counted like code words, with every 5 characters or fraction thereof treated as one word. (7) Punctuation marks, counted as one word each, are usually not typed in cablegrams.

How to Type Messages. You probably telephone many of your domestic and international wire messages to Western Union or one of the international carriers. But when you type telegram or cablegram copy for delivery, observe these guidelines and, preferably, use the printed forms provided free by Western Union: (1) Make an original and one copy for the recipient, one copy for your office files, and one copy for the accounting department. (2) Check the appropriate box to indicate which type of service (e.g., international service) you want and type the class (e.g., night letter) desired two spaces above the address. (3) Type a complete address, single spaced, sufficient for delivery at the destination, but omit the salutation and complimentary close. (4) Indicate the date and hour at the right margin across from the city and state. (5) In the lower left corner type the address and telephone number of the sender and the reference initials (if any) and show whether the message is sent paid, charge, or collect. For a charge, type the name of the charge account in the appropriate space on the form. (6) Type *AR* in the space provided if you want a reply and type *Report Delivery* if you want confirmation of delivery. (7) Use caps and lowercase throughout, except use all caps for code words. (8) Double-space the message body. (9) Type a separate list (Western Union has a form for this) of names and addresses if the message is to go to more than one person. (10) Generally, when typing words, symbols, and so on, observe the guidelines given above on how to count charges for telegrams and cablegrams.

Tips on Cost Control. The cost of wire services can get out of hand if you do not pay strict attention to time differentials and excess wordage. Some secretaries are careful to check time differences throughout the United States and overseas when placing telephone calls but fail to consider the effect of such variations in sending telegrams. As a result many telegrams are sent by the more costly fast-telegram or full-rate message class when, because of time differences, they will not reach the addressee until the following business day anyway. In other words, a careful check of time differentials would show when a message might just as well go by a less expensive class of service. (See the map of time zones in the Guide to Miscellaneous Data and, for international service, consult a published guide to time differentials worldwide.)

Since extra words mean extra cost, you can also avoid needless expense by carefully editing your messages. Wire messages do not have to be beautiful or delicate prose with complete, properly punctuated sentences. For instance, an opener such as "We would very much appreciate it if you would send us full details . . ." is a costly and unnecessary elaboration of a less expensive and brief statement such as "Please send full details . . . " or, even better, "Send full details. . . ." The trick is to examine every word and delete anything nonessential and to rephrase something whenever it can be said in fewer words.

Chapter 4
Applying Typing and Dictation Techniques

Most secretaries spend a lot of time at their typewriters, and some of this work involves transcribing machine dictation or shorthand notes. Good typing and stenographic skills are essential in almost all secretarial work. Equipment and methods may vary from office to office, but two things always enter into every picture: speed and accuracy. It is rarely a question of which is more important. A secretary, therefore, must learn and apply all available typing and dictation techniques that will enable her to process work quickly and handle a demanding work load while insuring the complete accuracy of each finished product. This may sound formidable, but the techniques discussed in this chapter reveal a surprisingly easy and enjoyable approach to your typing and dictation duties.

DEVELOPING SUCCESSFUL TYPING TECHNIQUES

There is more to typing than having good posture and maintaining the proper chair height, although such matters are important. To develop successful typing techniques, you need to observe certain rules and procedures, for example, how to (1) organize material to be typed; (2) make special characters; (3) type on forms and ruled lines; (4) handle miscellaneous material such as cards, labels, and envelopes; (5) type numbers and fractions; (6) make vertical rules; (7) feed numerous sheets; (8) make carbon copies; (9) make corrections; (10) type stencils; (11) space after punctuation marks; (12) type special material such as tables and reports; and (13) prepare material for printing. But before undertaking any of these things, you should become familiar with something else—your typewriter (see also chapter 6). Even the best techniques will fail if you do not know how to use your machine properly or if you do not keep it clean and in good working condition.

Organizing Your Material. In any job it helps to avoid disruptions after work has begun. If you have to stop what you are doing, get up, and start looking for something, time is lost, and the likelihood of making an error increases. This is especially true with typing. The best way to avoid such disruption is to have all your material organized in advance. This includes preparations for your machine. Be certain you have the right ribbon for the work you are doing and have all erasure and other correction materials within easy reach. Paper supplies should be arranged in your desk drawer—or placed on top of your desk—for easy selection and rapid insertion into the typewriter.

Check figures, the spelling of names, and so forth, *before* you start typing. However, you may want to have certain files and other reference material on your desk in case you discover something you overlooked earlier that needs verification. Also, before you start typing, estimate the length of the finished copy. This will suggest to you how much paper to have ready, whether to use a wide or narrow margin setting, and so on. If necessary, keep samples of different letters and text pages nearby. Mark them for wordage and size of margins and then use them as guides when estimating new material. The objective is to avoid having to retype something simply because it does not fit properly on the page.

How to Make Special Characters. Part of the task of becoming familiar with your typewriter involves determining what special characters are on your keyboard. Your typewriter, for instance, may have parentheses marks but no brackets. Perhaps it has an exclamation point, or perhaps you must improvise to make one. You need not be concerned if your machine lacks many of the special characters you occasionally need. By overtyping various standard letters and symbols (typing a letter, backspacing, and typing another letter on top of the first), you can create a sufficient likeness for most characters.

For example: (1) To make a *paragraph* mark, overtype a capital "P" with the lowercase letter "l" (℗). (2) For a *division* mark, combine a colon and a hyphen (÷). (3) An *exclamation* mark can be made with an apostrophe typed over a period (!). (4) Turn the cylinder slightly toward you and type a lowercase "o" to make a *degree* mark (º). (5) *Brackets* are made by using the diagonal and underscore keys (⌐). (6) One lowercase "s" over another, with the second slightly raised, makes a *section* sign (§). (7) The *equal* sign can be made with two hyphens, the second placed slightly above the first (=). (8) A lowercase "c" and a comma will make a *cedilla* (ç). (9) To make a *caret,* use the underscore and the diagonal (⁄). (10) A hyphen and diagonal will make a *plus sign* (≠). (11) The *pound sterling* sign can be made with a capital "L" and a hyphen (Ⱡ). (12) Use the apostrophe key for *minutes* (') and the quotation key for *seconds* ('').

Typing on Forms and Ruled Lines. The position of typed lines and even the individual letters in words can make a form look neat or messy. To avoid crooked lines of type and letters that cut across rules and boxes, follow these procedures: Adjust the form in your machine so the letters will strike slightly above the ruled lines. By using the variable line spacer, you can align the type so letters with tails (e.g., *y* and *p*) just touch the ruled lines. You may also need to shift the paper slightly left or right so your letters fall neatly within boxes on the form. Finally, adjust the paper if necessary to be certain that the lines of type will be straight and precisely parallel to the ruled lines.

When you must make carbon copies, forms can be troublesome if the copies are not carefully aligned, one back of another. The first thing to do is hold all of the copies up to the light and see if the rules on each sheet are aligned. Discard any form that appears out of alignment with the others. Before adding the carbon sheets between each form, insert the set of forms into the typewriter far enough to hold it securely. Then you can slip in the carbon sheets and roll the entire pack into place. Some secretaries make a final test of position by inserting a pin into all the copies through one of the ruled lines. If the copies are correctly aligned, the pin will stick through the same rule at the same place on each form.

Handling Cards, Labels, and Envelopes. A different approach is in order when you must position copy on odd-sized, sometimes bulky, material such as small cards, labels, and envelopes. Small cards, for instance, are more easily handled if you chain-feed them from the front of the platen, or roller. Be sure to insert each new card so its bottom is held in place by the card you just finished typing. Another possibility is to make a slit in a larger piece of heavy paper, wide enough to insert the bottom of the card into it. This will help hold the card steady while you roll all of it—paper and card—into your machine.

Envelopes are like cards in that they can be chain-fed through your machine. After you type the first envelope, roll it toward you until one-half inch shows above the alignment scale. Then insert another envelope from the front between the first envelope and the platen. Now you can roll the platen back to release the first envelope. This will bring the next one into position for typing. (Chain-feed from the back of the platen when envelopes have very thick or wide flaps.)

Large sheets of address labels that are torn off one by one after being typed will give you few problems. But it is not so simple when you have to insert and type one tiny label at a time. To cope with this problem, secretaries frequently make a one-inch fold across the middle or upper one-third of a sheet of paper. Once the paper has been rolled into the machine, with the folded edge up, it serves as a pocket into which you can tuck a small label and thus feed it through the machine and hold it in place along with the larger sheet.

Typing Numbers and Fractions. You may have many or few occasions to type numbers and fractions, depending on the kind of work your office handles. Either way, learning a few basic rules will take you through the most common situations. Fractions, for example, should always be typed the same. If you type some using the diagonal key (e.g., 1/6), type all of them that way (e.g., 1/6, 2/5, 1/2). Leave a space in a mixed fraction (e.g., 12 1/3). When you spell out the fractions, use a hyphen (e.g., one-fourth; twelve twenty-sevenths).

Numbers in nonscientific data are subject to one of two rules according to your office preference: (1) spell out numbers ten and below or (2) spell out numbers one hundred and below as well as all large round numbers such as two thousand. In either case, if you use a large number somewhere within a paragraph (e.g., 126), use numbers for everything else within that paragraph that refers to the same item, even figures of ten and below (e.g., 126, 7, 11). Roman numerals, however, are always typed using capital letters (e.g., XXVI), as shown in the Guide to Miscellaneous Data. (You will also find there a table of common percents and their fractional equivalents.)

When you use numbers in columns, align them by decimals, dollar signs, commas, and so forth (you can use your tabulator to make it easier to set up columns and tables):

$$\begin{array}{r} \$100.01 \\ 2.05 \\ \underline{.70} \\ \$102.76 \end{array}$$

However, align various figures at the left (or center them):

5%	5 percent
$70	seventy dollars
200 lbs.	200 pounds

Avoid dividing numbers at the end of a line of text. But if you must do this, divide the number after one of the commas and as close to the middle of the number as possible.

Making Vertical and Horizontal Rules. Some of the material you type may require horizontal and vertical rules. It is usually easy to make a horizontal rule with an electric typewriter simply by holding down the underscore key. However, the rule may appear slightly ragged or at least less precise than a fine rule made with pen and ink. Then there is the matter of making vertical rules, for example, between columns in a table. At some time you will probably have to make rules by some means other than a typewriter key.

Your typewriter may have a notch on its paper holder where you can insert a pen, pencil, or stylus (for a stencil). Or you may be able to use the fork of its ribbon guide. Before deciding where to insert the point, check your machine carefully so you do not puncture the ribbon. The object is to hold the pencil, pen, or stylus point firmly against the paper while it is in position in your typewriter. For a horizontal rule, you would then move the carriage from left to right. For a vertical rule, you would rotate the platen forward. Following this procedure, you should be able to produce clean and straight vertical and horizontal lines.

Feeding Numerous Sheets. Inserting and feeding an original and one or two carbon copies into your typewriter is seldom a problem. The difficulty arises when you must insert and feed through a large pack of sheets. For example, you might have to type a letter with six carbon copies, or you might have to prepare invoices with multiple copies, or you might have to work with a large pack of forms (see Typing on Forms and Ruled Lines, above). There are many possibilities, depending on the work your office handles. In most of these cases, the problem and solution are the same.

Many secretaries believe that the best procedure is to insert the sheets of paper first, slipping in the carbon sheets afterward. To do this, you would release the paper feed, insert the sheets of paper, return the release lever, and feed the paper far enough into the machine for it to be held securely in place. After that you can drop in the carbon sheets (carbon side toward you). Another possibility is to hold the entire pack stable by placing it under the flap of an envelope while inserting it, although you should double-check the alignment of the copies with this procedure. (See Handling Cards, Labels, and Envelopes, above, for tips on inserting and chain-feeding other items.)

Making Carbon Copies. In some organizations the office copier is used more and more to make copies, so carbon copies have become less common than they once were. But in many establishments the carbon copy still reigns supreme. The conscientious secretary, therefore, makes it a point to select the right carbon paper and use it to best advantage. For instance, **carbon** paper comes in different weights and colors. Common grades are light-weight (one to ten copies); medium weight (one to five copies); heavy weight (one to two copies); and plastic, or film (one to ten copies). Also, for certain jobs treated carbonless paper and carbon sets (paper and carbon sheet attached at the top) are popular.

The need to make carbon copies introduces a number of potential problems. One—feeding numerous sheets—was discussed in the previous section. Another familiar procedure involves typing on the carbon sheets themselves but not on the original while the entire pack is kept in the machine. The obvious solution is to place pieces of paper over the original and the other carbon sheets where you do not want the typing to appear. Type the information over those pieces of paper and then remove them. The typing will show only on the carbon sheets that did not have pieces of paper over them. To avoid making an indentation on the original during this process, some secretaries shift or remove the original and later replace it. But this practice must be undertaken cautiously or the lines of type on the original will be out of alignment after you return it to the machine.

Making Corrections. Some copy must be perfect. Certain legal documents, for example, cannot have erasures or other corrections. But most general material (e.g., correspondence and reports) is acceptable with an occasional inconspicuous correction. You may spot an error while your paper is still in the machine, or you may discover it later when proofreading. Erasing an error or blotting it out with correction fluid is sometimes easier when the paper is removed from your typewriter. However, after you return the paper to the machine, you must check the alignment. One way to do this is to set your ribbon on the stencil position and hit the correct key lightly. The slight indentation this makes will indicate if the alignment is off.

Numerous correction aids are available, and some machines have their own built-in correction device. Correction paper (tape) and correction fluid, available in different colors to match your stationery and typing paper, are both popular. When these supplies are used carefully and neatly, the corrections are reasonably inconspicuous. Some secretaries, though, believe that the right eraser (e.g., soft, hard, glass, electric, or art gum), used with

an eraser shield, makes the least notice-
able correction. However, care must be
exercised or the eraser will tear through
the paper. Material prepared for duplication, such as stencils, must be treated differently. To correct a stencil, for instance,
you would use a paper clip or burnisher to
close the perforations made by an incorrect letter, and then you would apply a
thin coat of correction fluid. Since there
are so many correction supplies on the
market, it is helpful to visit an office supply store and ask a salesperson to describe
the different types and uses of correction
materials.

Typing Stencils and Masters. Many offices have mimeograph machines, spirit
duplicators, or tabletop offset duplicators.
Some offices, however, prefer to send out
their duplicating work. Either way, you
should know how to prepare the stencils
and masters used for duplication. Before
you start typing a stencil, find out the
quantity of output needed and if the stencil must have drawings as well as typing
on it. Since there are several types of stencils, you must select the appropriate one
for the job. Before beginning, you also
may want to type a rough draft on regular

paper. When you are ready, clean the typewriter with type cleaner or a stiff brush, move the ribbon lever to the stencil position, and insert a cushion sheet between the stencil and its backing sheet. Type with a steady staccato touch at slightly less than your normal speed. Errors are corrected with a burnisher and fluid as described in Making Corrections, above.

Two common types of masters are spirit and offset masters. A spirit master set should be inserted into your typewriter open end first. Colored carbon, if used, should be inserted with the colored carbon face up. With your ribbon lever in the usual ribbon position, type with a steady staccato stroke at slightly less than your normal speed. To correct a spirit master, cover the error on the carbon side with self-adhesive correction tape and type over it again. You also could cut out the error and tape in a fresh piece of carbon. For an offset master (called a Duplimat), use an offset typewriter ribbon, an offset carbon ribbon, or a carbon ribbon. First clean the type and then use your normal touch but at a slightly slower speed. A special offset eraser should be used to make corrections on Duplimats.

Spacing After Punctuation Marks. Most of the rules for spacing after punctuation marks have evolved through usage and are widely accepted in the business world. Yet you can find many examples of incorrect form in typed copy as a result of carelessness or lack of knowledge. The one thing to keep in mind when following space rules is this: Do not separate a punctuation mark from the word it follows. A dash, for example, following a word that falls at the end of a line should be placed immediately after that word, *not* at the beginning of the next line of type.

Leave *no space* in these instances: (1) between any word and the punctuation that follows it, (2) before or after a dash, (3) between quotation marks and the quoted matter, (4) before or after a hyphen, (5) before or after an apostrophe (unless it begins or ends a word), (6) between items separated by a virgule (diagonal), (7) between the initials of an abbreviation such as a.m. or p.m., and (8) between parentheses (or brackets) and the matter they enclose.

Leave *one space* in these situations: (1) after a comma, (2) after a semicolon, (3) after a period following an initial (or an abbreviation), (4) after a suspended hyphen (e.g., the late- and early-blooming plants), (5) after an exclamation point in the body of a sentence, and (6) before and after "x" used as "by" (e.g., 4″ x 6″).

Leave *two spaces* in these instances: (1) after a period (or exclamation point or question mark) ending a sentence, (2) after a colon, and (3) after a figure or letter introducing an item in a list (e.g., 1. history; 2. math).

Typing Reports and Tables. Styles of special material such as reports and tables vary widely. When in doubt what to do, ask your employer or follow the established practice in your office. However, it may be up to you to set up such material according to generally acceptable guidelines. If so, keep in mind that your material must be presented in a neat, clear, and consistent format.

Formal *reports* are usually double-spaced (the informal memo is frequently single-spaced). The title page should give the report title, the date of the report, and the name(s) of the person(s) submitting it. A table of contents may be single-spaced if it is long. Center the contents material on the page, with chapter or topic numbers and titles to the left and page numbers to the right. Make your subheads consistent throughout the text. For example, if the first head for a major section is centered in all caps, type all heads for the other major sections centered in all caps, too. If the first subsection head is typed flush left in uppercase (capital) and lowercase (small) letters, type the other subsection heads the same way. Number footnotes consecutively from 1 on (or you may use symbols such as asterisks if there are only a few) and type each one single-spaced at the bottom of the page where the corresponding number appears in the text (or collect all of them at the end of the report). A bibliography is typed single-spaced at the end of the report. Consult the latest edition of a style book (e.g., *A Manual of Style,* University of Chicago Press) for examples of footnote and bibliography styles. Preliminary pages such as the preface and introduction, if any, are typed double-spaced the same as a regular text page. For instructions on copyrighting a report, contact the Register of Copyrights, Library of Congress, Washington, D.C. 20540.

Tables should be set up on separate pages. They are often single-spaced and, if there are many, you may want to number them from 1 on. At the appropriate place in the text there should be a reference to each table, for example, "see table 3" or "see Rotoblade Exports, 1975–80." One of the most common styles for tables has only horizontal rules—after the table title, after the row of column heads, and between the table body and the footnotes below it—with no vertical rules between columns. The row of cross heads is frequently typed, each centered above a column, in uppercase and lowercase letters, and the column of stub heads is typed flush left with an initial capital only in each entry. Finally, remember to line up statistics in the table columns by decimals and commas as described in Typing Numbers and Fractions, page 101.

Preparing Material for Printing. Many secretaries must type material to be submitted to a printer. To avoid errors and unnecessary expense, special care must be taken to prepare such copy properly and to submit it with clear instructions. A lot depends on whether you are typing finished copy that will be photographed and printed exactly as you have prepared it or whether the material must be typed and then submitted to a compositor (typesetter) who will set the finished copy from your typed manuscript. If your copy is to be photographed, it must be typed precisely as you want the finished product to look, without messy erasures or other corrections. On the other hand, if you want a compositor to set the copy, you must be certain to give full instructions about matters such as size and style of typeface for the heads, the body copy, the footnotes, and so on; the margin width; the amount of paragraph indentation; and for anything else that would affect the appearance of the material. Corrections are acceptable if they do not make it difficult for the compositor to read the manuscript. Costs may vary a great deal depending on the quantity of material needed, the type of job, and the firm handling the work. Thus it always pays to get two or three quotes from different printers before proceeding.

When a compositor sets the type from your manuscript, you may first receive galley proofs and then page proofs to proofread. With simple jobs, though, the compositor may skip the galley stage and go straight into pages. If not, the galleys will later be divided into individual pages of copy. Either way, the proofreading and marking of corrections on the proofs must be handled carefully or errors and omissions will appear in the finished product. Use the proofreader marks shown in the Guide to Miscellaneous Data when you correct the proofs. Remember that there is no charge for actual typesetting errors made by the compositor, but your employer *will* be charged for other revisions and changes made in the proof stage that are not compositor errors. Before you return the proofs to the compositor, double-check the margins; the spacing around heads, footnotes, and so on; the type size and faces (e.g., boldface, italic); the pagination; and any other item affecting the appearance or accuracy of the material.

HANDLING DICTATION AND TRANSCRIPTION

Taking dictation and transcribing it are two of the more common secretarial duties. Some employers still prefer to dictate in person, but machine dictation is rapidly growing in popularity. With machines, the employer can record from almost any location—in the office or a hotel room or from a car, airplane, or train—while the secretary is busy doing other things. The efficient secretary is able to handle both person-to-person dictation and machine dictation. She knows how to transcribe efficiently and accurately from both shorthand notes and dictation belts, discs, or tapes. (See chapter 6 for further details on dictation-transcription equipment.) The following discussion gives you tips on taking dictation and tells you how to transcribe notes and how to transcribe from a machine.

Tips on Taking Dictation. Your employer may call you in to take dictation on a moment's notice. To be prepared at all times, you need to keep certain materials well organized and readily available: a notebook, sharpened pencils and a fine-point pen, a red (or other color) lead pencil, rubber bands and paper clips, and a calendar. Depending on the work in your office, you may also need to retrieve various files and records to take along during dictation.

It helps to face your employer and place your notebook where you can write easily and turn pages rapidly. Keep a rubber band around the pages that are already filled. Date each dictation entry at the beginning and put the dictator's initials at the end. Then start recording in the left column. You may want to leave the right column blank if your employer tends to make a lot of changes or additions later. It is important to devise a system in advance for indicating words to be typed in all caps or underscored. For instance, two or three lines beneath a word might mean to type it in all caps and one line might mean to underscore it. Use the colored lead pencil to write all special instructions such as the number of copies and to whom. Take advantage of interruptions to review your notes for questions you may want to ask when your employer finishes each piece. (See also chapter 6 for examples of dictation shortcuts.)

How to Transcribe Notes. When you are ready to transcribe your notes, take time to review them and organize everything, including all materials and supplies you will need when typing each entry. If possible, transcribe your notes right after taking them, while everything is fresh in your mind. Be certain to verify names, addresses, dates, and so on, before you start typing. Similarly, make any grammatical corrections in advance. Consult your employer if you have any doubts about how much editing and polishing is expected of you. Do not hesitate to ask about anything that appears questionable. For example, your employer may have forgotten to mention something in one of the letters. Finally, make it a point to estimate the length of each piece before you start typing so it will be positioned properly on the page. Without such advance preparations you run the risk of having to retype some of your material. (See also Organizing Your Material, above.) Draw a diagonal red line through the notes of all entries that have been typed, signed, and mailed.

How to Transcribe from a Machine. Since many employers use dictating equipment at least some of the time (many of them, all of the time), you need to know how to transcribe belts, discs, and tapes (see chapter 6 for more about the equipment). The first order of business is to learn how to use the machines in your office. Once you are familiar with them, follow most of the same procedures applicable to the transcription of shorthand notes. That is, organize your materials; listen to the belt, disc, or tape; and check names, addresses, dates, and so on, for accuracy and omissions. Decide on any grammatical corrections and other editorial changes in advance. Listen to the special instructions and question anything your employer has forgotten. Many of the machines have devices that show how many words have been dictated, and this will help you estimate size and position the material properly on the page. When everything is signed, sealed, and mailed, draw a diagonal line through the identification strip that comes with belts and tapes.

Chapter 5
Streamlining Filing and Reminder Systems

Some secretaries are responsible for filing and finding only in their own office; others work with larger, more complex departmental files; and some secretaries handle the highly sophisticated storage and retrieval systems of a large, centralized filing department. One factor in particular is evident in each instance: a sound and efficient filing system is essential to insure that material can be retrieved rapidly. Sometimes the material concerns a matter that is pending. In other words, it must be followed up later. Along with sound filing practices, then, a secretary needs to have a reliable and effective reminder and follow-up system.

HOW TO USE EFFECTIVE REMINDER SYSTEMS

No one's memory is good enough to remember everything that has to be done tomorrow, next week, or next month. Without a good reminder system a secretary would be overwhelmed with such details. An effective reminder and follow-up system is the answer for a busy secretary. File folders, card files, and calendars are three common choices for the various types of reminder and follow-up activities. To be effective, however, each one must be referred to every day. But before you can handle such reminder and follow-up duties successfully, you need to know (1) how to use calendars for appointments and other reminders, (2) how to set up an effective follow-up system, and (3) how to use tickler card files.

Using Calendars for Reminders. Most secretaries—and executives—would agree that they cannot function without a calendar to remind them of upcoming events and work to do. Stationery and office supply stores have a variety of calendars, including the familiar desk calendar and the yearbook. The style you use depends on the type and amount of information you must record. If your employer has numerous appointments each day, you may want something that has 15- or 30-minute time intervals. Secretaries often prefer a desk style that shows each day's activities at a glance. If your calendar is truly to serve as a reminder system, you should go through the entire year and record not only appointments but other items such as anniversaries and birthdays, payment dates, renewal dates, and tax dates. In fact, make a note of each item a few days in advance, as well as on the date it occurs.

Your employer's calendar should also show appointments, meetings, and dates of other miscellaneous events—anything he or she should remember. Many executives like the bound yearbook style of calendar, but they often carry a small pocket calendar, too. Each morning, before your employer arrives, enter any new reminders on the calendar(s). Usually it is sufficient to enter the item on the date it occurs, without the advance notice you have on your own calendar. Some secretaries additionally type a 3- by 5-inch card of each day's activities for their employers. Whatever type of calendar you use in your office, be certain to keep it current and consult it daily.

How to Set Up a Follow-up System. It often seems that nothing is completed all at once. There is always something to do later, someone to contact later, or something you expect to receive later. When such matters involve correspondence and other documents, a follow-up system using file folders is helpful. You can arrange these folders almost any way that meets your needs. The idea is to put an extra copy of the correspondence or whatever needs later action in the follow-up files.

You might need a folder for each month and one or more for future years. Behind the folder for the current month, you could also place 31 additional folders, one for each day of the month. Then you would simply drop each matter needing follow-up in the folder marked for the day you want to take action. When that day comes, you would check the folder, handle the matter, and either complete it or put it in a new folder for later action. Each day you would check the current day's folder, and after it is empty, you would move it ahead to the next month. At the end of the month, then, all 31 folders would have been placed behind the file for the next month. This simplified system can be expanded or changed as you wish. The important thing is to have an accurate and reliable follow-up system that works for you and is appropriate for the material handled in your office.

Using Tickler Card Files. Many secretaries like to use a 3- by 5-inch card file to remind them of matters such as due dates and renewal dates where there is no correspondence to place in file folders. (Records pertaining to such matters are described in chapter 10.) Nevertheless, a card may refer to some document in the regular files, for example, an insurance policy. Should you have enough activity of this type to warrant maintaining a card file in addition to the file folder system of follow-up, you might use the same arrangement suggested in How to Set Up a Follow-up System, above. You would have 12 monthly guides, 31 daily guides, and 1 or more guides for future years. Each card would be filed back of the day when action is needed, and everything would be advanced the same as it is with a file folder system. To be reliable and useful, a card system—any follow-up system for that matter—must be consulted daily and kept current at all times.

HOW TO APPLY EFFECTIVE FILING TECHNIQUES

Many secretaries spend a substantial amount of time filing correspondence and other material and then retrieving it later for reference. When you think how much paperwork is generated in most organizations in one day alone, it is clear how important the filing and finding process is for both secretaries and their employers. To handle this function efficiently, a secretary needs to be familiar with (1) types of filing systems, (2) indexing and alphabetizing procedures, (3) containers and equipment, (4) preparation of material for filing, (5) cross-referencing, (6) control of material taken out, (7) retention and disposal procedures, and (8) advanced storage and retrieval methods.

Types of Filing Systems. The principal filing systems are (1) alphabetical, (2) subject, (3) numerical, (4) geographical, and (5) decimal. Your office may use one of these systems or some combination, for example, numerical-subject.

The *alphabetical system* is the most common filing system. Material is classified according to name and filed alphabetically (see Indexing and Alphabetizing Procedures, below). Even when other systems (e.g., numerical) are used, material within the various categories may still be alphabetized. A *subject file,* for instance, might be arranged alphabetically, although it also could be set up numerically or in any logical manner. This system is preferred when the subject (e.g., Management or Insurance) of the material, rather than someone's name, is more important. Subjects, of course, must be selected carefully so that everyone will find the files easy to use.

In certain situations one of the other systems might be better. A sales organization, for example, might want some type of breakdown by location—region, state, county, city, or whatever. A *geographical system* then would be ideal. When identification of material, people, and so forth, by number is common or when there are large numbers of items within some group, a *numerical system* is a logical choice. However, this system requires the maintenance of a separate alphabetical card index that identifies each numbered item (e.g., 10.217706 = John Smith). The *decimal system* follows the Dewey decimal system you see in some public libraries. All records are classified under no more than ten headings (000 to 900), with sub-headings subdivided numerically (e.g., 1 to 9, .1 to .10).

Indexing and Alphabetizing Procedures. Before you can alphabetize names for filing, you need to know how the names of people and organizations should be arranged on the file folder labels. Names of people are indexed by surname, then first name or initial, and next the middle or additional names and initials. John G. Jones would be indexed as Jones, John G. The firm name of John G. Jones & Son would be indexed as Jones, John G. & Son. But Hillcrest Community Church would be indexed as is: Hillcrest Community Church. When there is a common word such as *university* in the name, index according to the most distinctive word, for example, Wisconsin, University of.

Once you have your indexing rules established, alphabetize each item by the first word, then the second word, and so on. Disregard articles such as *the,* except in a foreign word, and disregard the ampersand symbol (&). But treat several successive letters (e.g., *ABC*) as a single word. Also, treat abbreviations as if they were spelled out (e.g., *St.* = *Saint*). Prefixes such as *De* or *Mac* are considered part of the surname. Numbers are alphabetized as if they were spelled out. Put titles (e.g., *Dr.*) in parentheses after the names. Hyphenated names representing two separate persons or units are handled as two words in a firm name, but a hyphenated individual name is treated as one word. A name that is sometimes written as one word, sometimes two, is then always indexed as one word. List a married woman by her husband's surname, next her first name, and finally her middle name (initial) or maiden name. Put her married name (e.g., Mrs. Mark Rogers) in parentheses below it. The following list gives you examples of many of these basic rules:

Arnold, A. T.

Astoria, Bank of

Decca, County of

De Vries, Peter

J & W Cleaning Co.

Jones, John G.

Jones, John Garvey

Jones Stationery Store

JVC Electronics

King, Maxine (Sr.)

Morris-Stone, Inc.

Morris-Ellerby, Harold M.

St. Peter's Cathedral

Sir Michael's Fashions

28 Murphy Street

Waterport News, The

Water Port Townhomes

Yarborough, Ellen R.
(Mrs. Henry K. Yarborough)

Authorities occasionally disagree about various indexing and alphabetizing rules. As always in these cases, the important thing is to be consistent in your use of whatever rule you adopt.

Containers and Equipment. The material you index and alphabetize obviously must go somewhere. A wide variety of filing containers, equipment, and supplies is available to fit almost any requirement you may have. There are various sizes and colors of labels, guides, folders, and dividing units. Similarly, there are containers of all types—trays, circular files, stackable and pullable drawer files, binder boxes, and visible card files, to name only a few. In large organizations the containers are often moved about by automated equipment (see Advanced Storage and Retrieval Methods, below). To get an idea of the many products designed to enhance and streamline your filing activities, write to manufacturers and visit company showrooms. Your local office supply store will no doubt have many new products to show you as well.

Preparing Material for Filing. You need to do more than index and alphabetize to get everything ready for filing. Some of your material may contain a number of papers that must be stapled together. Paper clips, rubber bands, and so on should then be removed. Torn papers must be repaired with tape. Each item thus needs to be examined and may require additional attention before it can be filed.

Some offices rubber-stamp material ready for filing with the word *FILE*. This helps secretaries rapidly segregate the material that has been released from that to be held. Further sorting of correspondence and documents will probably be necessary. Perhaps your office sends some material to a central file and retains other documents in the office. Or perhaps you use more than one type of file, for example, an alphabetical name file for correspondence and a subject file for other material. After everything is fully sorted and arranged, double-check your work once more and be certain you have prepared all cross-reference sheets that are needed (see Cross-Referencing, below).

Cross-Referencing. Sometimes when you have trouble deciding how to label a folder, it means that the material could logically be filed under more than one name or subject. The solution in such cases is to prepare a cross-reference sheet (or card). Cross-reference sheets are available from office supply stores, or you can type and then photocopy or mimeograph your own version. Each sheet should have space to type in (1) the name or subject of the cross-reference sheet, (2) what the material concerns, (3) the date of the material, and (4) the location of the material—what name or subject it is filed under. Many secretaries use different colored labels on folders containing cross-reference sheets. The label on a cross-reference folder might read:

Adams & Clark, Inc.
  see
Farnsworth Construction Co.

Although too many unnecessary cross-reference sheets would simply overcrowd the files, not enough could cause needless searching in the wrong places before finding a folder. It is usually preferable to risk having too many sheets than too few. In fact, there are times when material is referred to so often that it is better to photocopy the original material and keep duplicates, rather than cross-reference sheets, in the additional file folders.

Control of Material Taken Out. Many secretaries worry—with good reason—when other persons use the files, taking things out and putting them back, often in the wrong place. Clearly, when this situation exists, something has to be done to control it. Two common controls are the charge-out card and the out folder. A *charge-out card* is inserted where a folder or papers were removed. The borrower must fill in a tab that is attached at the top of the card (or the secretary completes it), showing various pertinent data such as (1) the name or subject, (2) the date of the material, (3) the name or initials of the borrower, and (4) the date borrowed.

When a borrower takes out an entire folder, it is usually preferable to insert an *out folder,* rather than a charge-out card, in the files. Then you can keep filing other correspondence even though the original folder is gone. Such folders also have a tab or card that the borrower must fill out similar to that used on a charge-out card. Many secretaries ask that material be returned to them rather than refiled by someone else. Some offices do not even allow others to remove original documents. The secretary instead makes a photocopy for the borrower. Follow the practice in your office, and when in doubt, ask.

Record Retention and Disposal. An organization needs to have a clear policy regarding the retention and disposal of records. This policy must be the secretary's principal guide in determining (1) what to keep, (2) how long to keep it, (3) what to dispose of, and (4) how or where to dispose of it. Federal and state laws govern what company records must be kept and for what time. Beyond that, company executives need to decide whether to retain material in the regular files, store it in inactive files, convert documents to microfilm or some other reduced form, and so on. When a policy is not clearly indicated, some secretaries type a checklist for their employers to complete—one column in which the secretary describes the type of record (e.g., minutes, invoices, personal correspondence, or contracts), another column where the employer can fill in the period each item is to be retained, and a third column where the employer can note where or how each item eventually should be stored or if it should be destroyed.

Advanced Storage and Retrieval Methods. Many organizations have too much paper to file and retrieve it manually. Machines are often needed to do a large portion of this work. (See also chapter 6.) Some equipment, at the push of a button, will move containers from large storage areas and return them again. Of course, automated processes do not always involve large, sophisticated machines. In other offices secretaries have smaller push-button filing equipment that revolves or that moves a tray or drawer in and out.

Another popular process is the reduction of information to a smaller size for storage. Certain material, for instance, may be put on punched cards or magnetic tape. Another process, microfilming, transfers information onto noncombustible film requiring minimal storage space. When anyone wants to see a certain document, a viewer with a screen is used to magnify the information for reading. With certain equipment, you can also make a photocopy at the same time. Most of these advanced storage and retrieval methods are more costly than regular filing methods—although with some there are savings in areas such as the cost of storage space—and organizations usually undertake a justification analysis before making a purchase.

HOW TO HANDLE PURCHASING AND STORAGE

Procedures differ when you must handle material other than letter- and legal-size correspondence and documents that belong in the regular files. Other items (e.g., miscellaneous forms, brochures, and stationery) must not only be stored but must be replenished at appropriate intervals. Usually such supplies are not put in the regular filing cabinets but are kept in central storerooms or office supply closets. Even in large organizations secretaries commonly retain an adequate supply of materials for daily use, sometimes organized on storage shelving for easy and quick selection. To handle your purchasing and storage duties properly, you must know how to (1) order and requisition supplies, (2) distribute supplies, and (3) store supplies.

Ordering and Requisitioning Supplies. If you work for a large organization, you probably get your supplies by filling out a requisition form and taking it to a central office that purchases, stores, and distributes materials to other employees. In a smaller organization, however, you may be expected to purchase whatever you need from local suppliers such as printers and office supply stores. In this case you may order and purchase materials using a petty cash fund, or you may charge the order to your employer's account. Either way, you must keep accurate and complete records of all expenditures. Also, whether you requisition supplies from a central department or purchase them outside your organization, it is necessary to plan ahead, monitor your usage closely, and reorder materials far enough in advance to be certain you do not run out. Many offices also like to plan their orders to take advantage of quantity discounts.

Distributing Supplies. When your supplies arrive, double-check your order against them as soon as possible—before anyone removes something. Discrepancies can be difficult, if not impossible, to verify once distribution has begun. After your order has been verified and the supplies are organized in your storeroom, supply cabinet, or some other storage area, you are ready to begin distribution.

Depending on the practice in your office, the use of supplies may be controlled or open. For example, one person may strictly supervise the distribution of supplies or others in the office may be permitted to help themselves. The advantage of controlled distribution is obvious. You can monitor what goes out, how often, and to whom. It is then easier to plan ahead and reorder materials in adequate time before they are depleted. If other employees are permitted to help themselves, you may want to keep a logbook in the supply area, where each person records what he or she removes and the quantity taken. This will give you an up-to-date checklist from which to compute totals and determine a reorder date for each item.

Storing Supplies. It is often the secretary's job to store the supplies used in the office. The overall task of purchasing and storage will be much more manageable if you keep a well-organized and orderly supply area. Several organizational practices are helpful. For instance, you should keep individual items grouped together— stationery in one place, invoices in another place, and so on, using dividers if necessary to separate one thing from another. Keep paper clips and other small items in boxes. Open shelving makes it easier to spot items quickly, although even then you should label different compartments or sections. Whether you use closed or open storage space, keep the items you use most often where you can reach them without difficulty. For each item store new packages behind the older ones. Mark the original quantity on outside wrappers or boxes (if any) and change it to the current quantity whenever something is removed. Above all, keep a record of what you have on hand and periodically check the quantity on hand so you will know when to reorder before the supply of any item is exhausted.

Chapter 6
Improving Office Efficiency and Organization

Experts in management and administration often say that the secret to success is knowing how to control a situation and not letting it control you. Secretaries, however, sometimes think they have no choice but to accept the cumbersome, ineffective, and inefficient practices and procedures dictated by their employers. In reality there is a great deal that secretaries can do to improve office efficiency and organization, and most employers are eager to hear valid suggestions in this area. In almost any situation, you can find many opportunities to do your part in applying timesaving techniques and learning how to make good use of the machines and systems in your office.

ESTABLISHING BETTER PROCEDURES

Without effective and efficient practices and procedures, everyone in an office—not just the secretary—runs the risk of getting caught in an avalanche of paperwork and confusion. Without good procedures, then, productivity will decline or, at best, fail to increase significantly. Since the secretary is such a vital link in the office chain, she must do what she can to improve office efficiency and organization. This means (1) planning ahead and organizing her work load, (2) using shortcuts in common tasks such as typing and filing, (3) making the office layout more effective, and (4) using forms and other time-saving materials.

Planning and Organizing Your Work Load. How do you spend your time at work? The question is not as simple as it sounds. Nor is the answer. One way to approach the matter of planning and organizing your work is to do a preliminary study. For two weeks write down everything you do (process mail, answer the phone, greet visitors, file, and so on), when you do it, and how long it takes. This will give you an idea of how you spend your time, what tasks are predominant, and whether the tasks appear haphazard and scattered throughout the day or well organized. If you have assistants, ask them to keep the same type of record.

After keeping track of time usage for two weeks, analyze the results and look for obvious patterns. Do particular jobs (e.g., sending bills) fall on certain days each week or month or on certain hours each day? Would it be easier and more efficient to do these things another time or all at once rather than a little here and a little there? Do you have slow periods when you might plan on odd jobs such as cleaning out the files and updating mailing lists? Are there times when you have fewer interruptions during the day and thus could best do things such as transcribe dictation? Are you doing things that really should be delegated to your assistants? Once you know the pattern of your work load, you can more easily plan and organize it—and that of your assistants—to ensure maximum effectiveness and efficiency.

Using Shortcuts to Increase Efficiency. It makes no sense to continue doing things the hard way or the long way when there are so many simple shortcuts. Chapter 2, for instance, explained how to speed the inserting process when handling outgoing mail. Chapter 4 explained how to chain-feed envelopes when typing rather than run them through the typewriter one at a time. All of the chapters have described effective procedures that will help you avoid time-consuming mishaps and errors. You can learn many additional timesaving techniques from others in your office and from books such as this. Better yet, you can devise your own time-savers from experience.

The list of available shortcuts is long. Fortunately, many special timesaving measures are available in routine areas such as typing and filing. For example: (1) Color coding of cabinets, books, file folder labels, carbon paper, and so on will help you find something you are searching for in less time. (2) Pressure-sensitive labels and envelopes can be handled faster than those you must pause to moisten. (3) You can flip the pages of your shorthand notebook more rapidly if you use a rubber finger. (4) Folding over the corner of a page in your shorthand notebook will make it easier to locate something you need to keep referring to. (5) If you insert envelopes to the left of the paper guide, between your letter and the platen, you can type an address without changing your left margin stop. (6) Always file with the latest material on top so that the most current information is readily accessible. All of these ideas are only a few examples of the many techniques you can use every day to save time and energy and, best of all, to make your job more enjoyable.

Improving the Office Layout. If you are always bumping into something on the way to a file cabinet, or if you constantly have to weave a path around various objects in your work area, something is wrong. Even if you have not been conscious of an obstacle course, the office layout may not be as good as it should be. In any organization wasted steps mean wasted time, and wasted time means wasted money. Probably no one is better qualified than a secretary to evaluate the office layout and suggest necessary improvements.

Some changes can be made without consulting your employer. For instance, is your dictionary within easy reach on your desk? Do you have a memo pad readily available by your telephone? Are the supplies you use regularly stored where you can reach them easily? People are creatures of habit, and it is all too easy to adjust to inconveniences. In an office—or anywhere—this is a mistake. It is worth the time and effort to examine all aspects of your office layout and make whatever improvements are desirable and useful.

Using Forms to Save Time. Can you imagine operating a business without forms to use for tasks that are constantly repeated? Invoices, applications, message slips, travel expense vouchers, subscription notices, cross-reference sheets, requisitions, and hundreds—even thousands—of other items would have to be typed from scratch each time. Although an abundance of such timesaving forms does exist, or could be devised, secretaries still type many items over and over. This is clearly wasted time and energy.

You may not be able to find the precise forms you want for your work already printed and for sale commercially. But most secretaries agree that they could create their own forms and duplicate them by mimeograph machine or office copier. However, many secretaries say that they are uncertain how to set up a form or what work might be handled best by forms. There are several easy ways to inspire your imagination: (1) Browse at length in an office supply store. (2) Ask or write for copies of office supply catalogs that contain forms. Some companies specialize in producing forms, and your local office supply dealer can give you the names of these firms. (3) Examine some current secretarial books, most of which give numerous examples of forms you should use. (4) Ask friends for samples of the forms they use in their departments or companies. (5) If your office has a forms file, look at the forms already in use to see which could be revised for another purpose. (If you do not have a forms file, start one.) (6) Observe how and why some forms are easier to type than others—the spacing of lines matches the spacing on your typewriter, instructions on the form are clear but concise, the size is right for your file folders, adequate space is provided to fill information in, and so on.

USING EQUIPMENT TO INCREASE EFFICIENCY

There is no doubt that machines save time. But needs vary greatly from office to office, and equipment—like time—costs money. Your employer will therefore want to be certain a machine is worth the cost before bringing it into your office. One of the most immediate concerns of the secretary is learning how to make good use of the machines that are already there. It is surprising how many machines are underused simply because someone failed to learn how to operate them. Learning what a machine will do and how to operate it is essential, of course. But you also need to know how to maintain the machine, what service agreements to arrange, and so forth. A number of machines are familiar sights in many offices: (1) electric, automated, and electronic typewriters; (2) dictation-transcription machines; (3) calculators and computers; (4) addressing and mailing equipment; (5) copying and duplicating equipment; (6) information storage and retrieval systems; and (7) miscellaneous aids such as electric letter openers.

Electric, Automated, and Electronic Typewriters. Today's typewriters are almost miracle workers. Each year manufacturers present some new feature, such as a built-in correction device, designed to make your job easier and help you do it faster. The *electric typewriter* is now commonplace, offering fast and simple operation and quality output. *Automated typewriters* can store information on magnetic cards or tape and print it out later at high speed. The *electronic typewriter* automatically performs many routine typing functions such as centering and underscoring. It can store phrases and later type them out automatically. In short, the new breed of typewriters takes the drudgery out of typing and frees the secretary to use more creative and productive skills.

Dictation-Transcription Machines. Dictating machines and transcriber units are so popular today that your employer probably has such equipment even if he or she actually prefers dictating to you in person. Using machines, your employer can dictate from any location, even while driving a car or taking a commuter train to work. One of the principal advantages is that the secretary is free to do other work while her employer is dictating. The dictating and transcriber units—as well as the combination models—are easy to operate. They come in all types and sizes, from large stationary models with numerous features and high-quality voice reproduction to miniature, pocket-size units that can be easily transported almost anywhere. They may operate with discs, belts, cassettes, minicassettes, cartridges, or some other recording media. Many offices choose a system that will be compatible with other systems used throughout the organization.

Calculators and Computers. Whether your office has no more than a small adding machine or there is a sophisticated computer complex, you need to know something about this type of equipment. Calculating machines that add, subtract, multiply, and divide have become increasingly widespread. Many offices have at least one of the quiet, desk-top electronic calculators—the type where numbers are illuminated on a small screen. Some employers also carry a miniature, pocket-size model wherever they go. Offices that are involved in accounting work often have larger machines, such as the printing calculator—the type where results are printed out on a roll of white paper tape. There are models to choose from to fit almost any requirement. Small computers, too, are becoming popular, and it is no longer surprising to find one in someone's office. These machines can store and process all kinds of information—payroll records, credit data, and sales-marketing information, to name only a few.

Addressing and Mailing Equipment. Organizations that do a lot of mailing need some addressing and mailing equipment, possibly a lot of it. Addresses can be maintained in many different ways. For very small lists, some secretaries type labels on multiple carbon sets. Offices that have automatic typewriters may keep certain lists on magnetic tape or cards. Other machines prepare metal address plates or address cards. The choice of equipment depends on many factors—size of list, frequency of use, imprint quality needed for the address, and so on. The choice of mailing equipment, too, depends on your needs. There are collating machines that automatically arrange papers into sets, large stapling machines, and folding and inserting machines. Even small offices, or those that do not handle large mailings, may have at least postage meter equipment that automatically stamps and seals each envelope. These machines are leased from the Postal Service and must be set by a postal clerk for the amount of postage you purchase.

Copying and Duplicating Equipment. You may use a local printer for much of your printing work, or you may go out to get photocopies made. But almost every office or department has a photocopier today, and many also have some type of duplicating equipment (e.g., a mimeograph machine). Copying machines come in a variety of sizes and differ in speed of output, quality of copies, and so forth. Different duplicating machines fit different needs. An offset duplicator, for instance, can produce as many as 5,000 copies from one offset master. The quality of reproduction is superior to that of the spirit duplicator or the mimeograph machine. Like many office machines, copiers and duplicators may be leased as well as purchased.

Information Storage and Retrieval Systems. Many organizations need advanced equipment to file and retrieve data (see chapter 5). Computers, of course, have a memory function and thus have storage capability. Information is first converted into a form suitable for computer storage, and it then can be recalled later when needed. Information can also be transferred onto magnetic tape, punched cards, microfilm, and other types of special storage material. Sometimes the data first must be converted into code or some other form, depending on the storage media being used, and then it is printed out later as needed. Information that is transferred to microfilm or a similar process is reduced in size for storage, and later, when retrieved, it is magnified to normal size for reading. Other equipment is designed simply to transport actual filing containers or file folders in and out of storage bins. Information storage and retrieval systems vary in size, cost, principal function(s), and available features. But all office machines have one thing in common: they will save you time and effort and thus bring you closer toward your goal of improving office efficiency and organization.

Miscellaneous Office Aids. Secretaries often overlook the smaller machines and devices that are available. These miscellaneous office aids can also help you improve your efficiency in the office. Electric letter openers, for instance, are great time-savers for the secretary who must open a lot of mail. Similarly, you can date the incoming mail much faster with a date stamper than by writing the date on each piece by hand. If you spend a great deal of time keeping pencils sharpened both for meetings and general office work, an electric pencil sharpener will make this task easier and less time-consuming. Secretaries who file a substantial amount of material each day can save time by using sorting trays and racks. Your local office supply store has these and many more timesaving machines and devices that can help you reduce the time you spend each day on so-called nuisance tasks.

Chapter 7

Arranging Meetings and Making Travel Plans

Preparations for meetings and travel frequently go hand in hand. Several persons may be involved in making the necessary plans, including your employer. But it is usually the secretary who handles most, if not all, of the preliminary arrangements. One thing is certain: executives must consult with each other to conduct their business, and thus they must attend many meetings of all sizes in various locations. When these meetings are held outside your organization, travel enters the picture. Either way, the secretary often plays a key role in arranging such meetings and in making the appropriate travel plans.

HOW TO HANDLE PREPARATIONS FOR A MEETING

The preparations for a small staff conference or a meeting with clients are not the same as the preparations for a large convention. Although a secretary may be expected to help prepare for a convention (type letters of invitation to speakers, get luncheon tickets printed, receive and acknowledge incoming registrations, and so on), many other persons are also involved. For example, there may be a committee appointed to set up the program, someone to work with the hotel staff at the convention site, and numerous other persons to handle the details peculiar to a large convention. But there may be few persons—perhaps none—to help you make preparations for a small meeting. Thus it is important to become familiar with (1) typical meeting arrangements, such as preparing a meeting room and notifying participants; (2) secretarial duties during a meeting, such as relaying messages and providing refreshments; and (3) special procedures for taking and typing the meeting minutes.

Preparing for the Meeting. Certain things must be done in advance to insure that everything is ready at the scheduled time. After the decision is made to have a meeting, the next thing to be decided is who will attend and where they will meet. Your employer will give you the names of the participants, and it will be your responsibility to notify each. A typical procedure is to telephone each person and confirm that the time, day, and place are acceptable to everyone. If they are not, your employer will have to suggest an alternative schedule, and you will again have to telephone each participant. After the time, day, and place are set, you should put a note on your calendar to follow up the calls with a memo, letter, or printed meeting announcement to each person. Also, put a notice of the meeting on your employer's calendar.

The next order of business is to reserve a meeting room in the city selected for the meeting site. If some participants must come by air travel, a hotel or motel near the airport would be a good location. If the meeting is to be a dinner meeting or luncheon meeting, the hotel or motel should be one that can handle your needs in meal planning and service. Your employer may also ask you to have the hotel reserve a block of rooms for the participants who will stay overnight. It may also be your responsibility to set up the meeting room just before the participants arrive. What you do depends on the type of meeting it will be. If special equipment and visual aids are needed, you must reserve such items in advance and see that they have been delivered and set up before the meeting begins. Check the number of chairs, the lighting, and the air conditioning or heating. See that there are ashtrays, sharpened pencils and pads, enough glasses and a pitcher of water, and a place for participants to leave their coats and other articles. If you are to serve something such as coffee and rolls, be certain the establishment providing the refreshments is prepared to deliver what you need in time for you to set it up in a convenient spot, perhaps just outside the door of the meeting room.

Another important preparation involves the agenda and other meeting materials your employer will need to take along. You will no doubt type the preliminary agenda and see that it is sent to each person in sufficient time before the meeting. It is often distributed with the meeting announcement. Your employer may want to ask each person to suggest (by telephone or letter) other topics to add to the final agenda that will be distributed at the meeting. As soon as you know what topics are on the agenda, you can begin collecting pertinent information for your employer. For instance, if one topic is the renewal of an insurance contract, your employer may want to take along the current insurance file. Some material should be given to your employer well in advance so he or she can study it and be prepared for discussion at the meeting. Finally, be certain your employer has pen and ink, notepaper, paper clips, a calendar, and any other miscellaneous supplies that may be needed during the meeting.

Special Duties During the Meeting. You will need someone to cover your telephone if you must attend a meeting to take notes, serve refreshments, or help in some other way. Whether you or someone else receives calls, the question may arise whether to interrupt a meeting to give someone a message. The usual practice is to handle calls yourself whenever possible or to take messages that can be given to someone after the meeting. But if there is an emergency, type the message, quietly hand it to the appropriate individual in the meeting room, and wait to see if he or she wants you to handle anything further. If you are in the meeting room taking notes (see Taking and Typing the Minutes, page 159), give these same instructions to the person who is answering your telephone for you.

It may be your responsibility to take care of miscellaneous duties during a meeting, for example, running errands, looking for something in the files, and serving refreshments. Light refreshments such as coffee and rolls (be certain there are napkins, cream, sugar, and so on), ordered in advance, should be delivered at the time you specify. In the morning participants may break anywhere between 10:00 and 11:00 and in the afternoon, between 3:00 and 4:00—whenever there is a logical pause in the meeting discussion. Many secretaries have everything set up on a table in an adjacent room or lobby so the meeting participants can serve themselves whenever they decide to interrupt their discussion. When the meeting is being held in a motel or hotel, the refreshments will probably come from within that facility. But when the meeting is being held in another type of facility—one that does not provide refreshments—you will have to place your order with a nearby delicatessen or restaurant that delivers. Some companies, of course, have their own internal food service.

Taking and Typing the Minutes. Before you take notes at a meeting, find out whether you should simply summarize general information for your employer or whether you should record full notes that will represent the official minutes of the meeting. Ask whether verbatim notes are required for motions, resolutions, and any controversial discussions. If they are, you may want to use a tape recorder to back up your shorthand notes. Whether your notes must be verbatim or a general summary of the proceedings, it is important to be alert throughout the entire meeting and record names and discussions accurately. If you miss anything, signal the chairman right away. Some secretaries prepare a seating chart to use in identifying each person who speaks. Preprinted resolution forms are also helpful. You can make up a form that has words such as *WHEREAS, RESOLVED, RESOLVED further,* and so forth positioned with adequate surrounding space so you can quickly fill in the details. Remember to record attendance in the beginning and note when the meeting is called to order and when it is adjourned. Keep the agenda, copies of reports, and other available material nearby so you can draw facts and figures from them as needed. Reports such as the treasurer's report are usually either summarized from the discussion or written in advance by the appropriate person and then attached to the minutes in that form.

After the meeting you should type the minutes as soon as possible. Usually a rough draft is submitted first (e.g., to your employer or to the chairman) for approval before the final copy is typed. Use the form preferred by your organization or, if there is none, follow these rules: (1) Center the heading—the group's name and the kind of meeting—in all caps and beneath that center the date in uppercase and lowercase letters. (2) In the first paragraph give the day, date, hour, place, name of the presiding officer, and type of meeting. After that the names of participants, present and absent, may be typed as lists in two or three columns. Specify if a quorum was present. (3) Double-space the text, with a triple space between each new item of business, but single-space resolutions. (4) Indent paragraphs 10 spaces and resolutions 15 spaces. (5) Capitalize *RESOLVED* and *WHEREAS*, and capitalize *BOARD OF DIRECTORS* and *CORPORATION* when these words refer to the group or organization holding the meeting. (6) Spell out sums of money and then put the figures in parentheses immediately after the words. (7) Use the past tense throughout, with complete sentences. (8) Make signature lines at the end for the secretary and the chairman to sign the minutes. (9) Attach appropriate reports and other documents before placing the final minutes in the minute book. (10) Make corrections that are introduced at the next meeting by drawing a line in ink through the copy and writing the correction above the error (or attach a separate sheet and refer to the sheet where the error is crossed out).

HOW TO MAKE TRAVEL ARRANGEMENTS

Travel is a way of life for many business and professional persons. Some go no farther than a nearby city, but others go to various foreign countries on a regular basis. If your employer travels even occasionally—for business or pleasure—you should be familiar with the usual procedures for making travel arrangements. To handle the basic steps involved in planning a trip, you need to know (1) how to make reservations and use a travel agency, (2) how to prepare an itinerary and organize material to take along, (3) how to handle foreign travel arrangements, and

(4) what to do when you travel with your employer.

Making Reservations. Before you can make reservations, you need to know the policy of your organization regarding things such as advances for travel expenses and the use of credit cards. (Your company may have a form that your employer must complete and submit before a cash advance can be secured.) You also need to know what type of accommodations your employer prefers, whether he or she likes to have a rental car waiting at each stopover, and so on. Once these things are clear, you are ready to make the reservations. Although you may have time to write a letter for each reservation (see chapter 9), there will be occasions when time is too short for this. Many secretaries therefore make their initial contacts with the hotel and airport or train station by telephone (or telegraph). At this time they ask the reservation clerks to confirm the reservations immediately by wire. Even when there is sufficient time to write letters, car rentals are usually handled by telephone, although a letter or wire confirming the arrangement may be sent immediately following the call.

Travel agents are almost always used

for foreign travel and frequently for domestic travel as well. Your telephone directory Yellow Pages will have a list of local agents (or you may request a list from the American Society of Travel Agents, 360 Lexington Avenue, New York, New York 10017). Large companies may have their own transportation office or department. Whether you make the reservations yourself or contact someone else who will make them, you must know what type of arrangements your employer wants. This means that you must collect adequate information in advance: exact travel dates, specific car rental needs, type of overnight accommodations desired, arrival and departure times, type of transportation (e.g., airplane or train) desired, and preferred class of travel for air service or room accommodations for train service.

Tickets may be purchased by check at the terminal or by mail when time permits. However, most persons use company charge accounts or personal credit cards, and the secretary simply gives the number of the card or account and the holder's name to the reservation clerk at the time the reservation is made. If reservations are changed or cancelled, full details must be given to the clerk along with a request for credit or a refund. Information about rates, schedules, and routes may be obtained from your organization's own transportation office (if any) or by checking timetables and contacting travel agents, airlines, Amtrak or other railroad agents, car rental agencies, local auto clubs or the nearest office of the American Automobile Association, and various hotels and motels. Your local library or a local travel agent may also have copies of motel and hotel directories and airline and railway guides (see chapter 11).

Preparing the Itinerary. Travel arrangements are seldom definite right away. Thus you should first prepare a tentative itinerary, showing a proposed schedule of (1) places to be visited, including dates and times of departure and arrival; (2) available hotel accommodations; (3) available car rental facilities; and (4) proposed air and rail reservations at each point of departure and arrival. This tentative plan will provide enough information for your employer to decide whether changes are needed or whether you may proceed with definite reservations.

When you are preparing the tentative itinerary, type an appointment schedule, too. Show every appointment planned during the trip, including (1) the name, title, firm, address, and phone number of each person to be visited; (2) the date and time of each appointment; and (3) comments concerning the type of appointment (e.g., dinner) and the purpose (what will be discussed). This is also a good time to begin collecting the materials your employer should take along. The appointment schedule will suggest reports, correspondence, and other items your employer may need for each visit. Put materials for each appointment in separate folders to avoid confusion. In another separate packet assemble all miscellaneous supplies: paper clips and rubber bands, pen and ink, stationery, postage stamps, business cards, checks, expense forms, timetables and maps, dictating belts or tapes, and so on.

The final itinerary should be prepared in triplicate. The original is for your employer, one copy is for you, and one copy is for your employer's family. Type the appropriate heads across the top of the page and list the information beneath them in column fashion. For example: *FROM* (city), *TO* (city), *VIA* (name of airplane or train), *DEPARTURE* (date and time), *ARRIVAL* (date and time), *ACCOMMODATION* (flight or train number), *CAR RENTAL* (type of car and location), *HO-*

TEL (name, address, and checkout time). Indicate at the top of the form whether the times shown are eastern, central, mountain, or Pacific and whether they are daylight or standard.

Handling Foreign Travel. Travel agents are indispensable in making arrangements for travel in a foreign country. They have up-to-date information on international transportation services (air, rail, and steamship), hotel facilities, car rental agencies, customs rules and regulations, passport and visa requirements, foreign currency needs, required vaccination certificates, foreign social customs, and points of interest to visit. In other words, you can find out everything you need to know in one place rather than face the formidable task of contacting numerous organizations and persons to collect data and make reservations on your own.

Even though a travel agent will make all reservations and arrangements, as well as give you any additional information you need about a proposed trip, you need to make certain preparations yourself. First, you need to collect all available information from your employer: who is going and reason for the trip; dates; destinations and stopovers; any preferences in type and class of transportation and sleeping accommodations; need for foreign currency, credit cards, travelers' checks, or letters of credit; interest in sightseeing excursions or other special arrangements; and anything else pertinent to the travel arrangements or the business to be conducted on the trip. The portion of this information pertaining to the travel itself must be organized clearly and accurately, typed, and presented to the travel agent. After that the agent may request further facts or ask you to check certain things with your employer. Just as you would do for domestic travel, you should prepare a preliminary itinerary, a final itinerary, and an appointment schedule for foreign travel (see Preparing the Itinerary, above). In addition, a foreign itinerary would state facts for each destination concerning customs, passport or visa requirements, vaccinations, and currency—and any other data peculiar to foreign travel. Holidays, for instance, differ from country to country, an important detail to consider when scheduling appointments.

Secretaries often do one other thing when making foreign travel plans—collect data relevant to the commercial aspect of the trip. Your travel agent will be able to advise you concerning commercial travel restrictions. In addition, you can prepare files of correspondence and other material that will be needed for each visit, request letters of introduction for your employer from banks to their foreign offices, help prepare introductory letters to persons your employer will visit overseas, collect basic data on business and trade in each country, secure a letter from your organization's president authorizing your employer to conduct business for the firm, advise the International Travel Officer at the Department of Commerce of your employer's itinerary and plans, and so on. Ask your employer whether there is anything further he or she will need.

Traveling with Your Employer. Some employers conduct so much business while traveling that they need a secretary en route. Whether this happens occasionally or frequently, you need to be prepared for possible travel with your employer. Matters involving reservations and appointments are handled just as you handle them for your employer. Assuming you will be going at the same time to the same place, simply make each reservation for two instead of one. Since your organization pays for your transportation, sleeping accommodations, and so on, each item will probably be handled exactly as it is for your employer—by completing a form to secure advance authorization for travel funds, by charging things to your company's travel account or your employer's credit card, or by some other procedure your employer instructs you to follow. However, like your employer, you must pay for your own after-hours entertainment and any personal purchases. Keep track of all legitimate travel and business expenses, using the same procedure your employer follows in submitting his or her travel expense reports. (Use company forms, if any, for such reports or ask your local office supply store for standard travel expense report forms.)

When you are traveling with an employer, matters of etiquette usually raise more questions than procedures for making reservations or handling expenses. When a female secretary travels with a male employer, she may wish to advise room reservation clerks of this and request rooms on different floors or at least not adjoining. Dictation should be taken in the hotel lounge or in a sitting room adjoining your employer's bedroom. However, you may do any necessary typing in your own bedroom (make advance arrangements for a typewriter through the hotel). Most secretaries work each day as usual while traveling, and thus business clothes are needed during the day. One or two outfits to wear to dinner are also a good idea. You will know in advance if formal evening wear is required for something such as a banquet. The less you can manage with, the better. Be prepared to find your own activities after hours, since your employer is not required to accompany you to dinner or nonbusiness events. In fact, he or she will probably be busy with clients in the evening as well as during the day.

Chapter 8
Learning to Write Correctly

Most organizations depend heavily on successful communications to accomplish their objectives. Thus it is easy to see why learning to write effectively is essential in almost every type of secretarial work. Not only should you be able to correct obvious grammatical and structural errors in your employer's letters, memos, reports, and so forth, but you should also be able to compose effective and productive written communications on your own. This means that you must use proper punctuation, learn correct spelling and word division, and master the basic rules of capitalization. (Chapter 9 discusses current letter-writing practices.) The following sections reflect current trends in writing style. However, since such matters change with time, you should make it a habit periodically to review the latest edition of a good style book such as *A Manual of Style* (University of Chicago Press).

USING PROPER PUNCTUATION

A skilled writer uses punctuation to good advantage. The obvious intent is to help readers follow a writer's thoughts and interpret them clearly and accurately—to lead readers through a maze of words that might appear jumbled and incoherent without proper punctuation marks. But punctuation can do more than lead readers and clarify thoughts. It can emphasize or deemphasize something. It can create impressions such as amazement (!) or doubt (?). Meanings can even be changed entirely simply by moving a comma. A careful writer uses punctuation correctly; a skilled—and careful—writer uses punctuation correctly and advantageously. Fourteen common marks of punctuation are described below: apostrophe, brackets, colon, comma, dash, ellipses, exclamation point, hyphen, leaders, parentheses, period, question mark, quotation marks, and semicolon.

Apostrophe. The *apostrophe* is used primarily to show possession, to show that letters or figures have been omitted, and to show the plural of numbers, letters, symbols, and abbreviations. Either an apostrophe and an *s* or an apostrophe alone is added, as shown below:

David's car	books' binding (more than one book)
Susan and David's car	
John Wilson's house	two cents' worth
	anyone's
the Adamses' party	it's (it is)
book's binding (one book)	August '81 (1981)
	p's and q's

In certain cases the apostrophe is omitted. For instance, you should not use an apostrophe to show the possessive case of personal pronouns. In other instances it has simply become common practice to drop the apostrophe:

The prize is yours.
Citizens Bank and Trust Company
1970s

Brackets. Some secretaries use parentheses in place of *brackets* when their typewriter does not have a bracket key. However, you can improvise to make brackets (as described in chapter 4) by using the diagonal and underscore keys. This will enable you to use brackets to enclose comments or corrections in quoted material and to enclose additional parenthetical material within parentheses. Brackets are particularly common in technical material. Mathematical expressions, for instance, frequently require parentheses, brackets, and other enclosures. Secretaries who work in offices that deal with such material must be familiar with a much wider use of brackets. The following are examples of the most common uses:

"The law [repealed in 1978] requires full compliance with this ordinance."

in standard size (also legal [8 1/2 × 14] size) letterhead

$[a(s - 1)(a - b)sa]$

Colon. You most often see the *colon* used to introduce a list or some type of series. But sometimes it is incorrectly used to introduce a series of items within a sentence following a form of the verb *to be*. It is incorrect to use a colon after *are* in this example: "The basic steps are: gather information, update information, and store information." But the following usage is correct:

The basic steps are:
1. Gather information
2. Update information
3. Store information

Introductions that take a colon are easy to recognize, for instance:

> The following are basic examples:
> These requirements must be met:
> Follow these four simple steps:

The colon is also used to indicate time, in biblical references, after salutations, and in footnotes:

> 10:30 a.m.
> Matthew 2:1
> Dear Mike:
> Mary A. De Vries, *Follett Vest-Pocket Secretary's Handbook* (Chicago: Follett Publishing Company, 1980).

Comma. One of the most widely used marks of punctuation is the *comma*. Although the trend is to use less punctuation in sentences, the comma is still necessary to separate certain phrases and words. These are common examples:

> I bought a dress, hat, and coat. (serial comma)
> Yes, it is true. (after an introductory expression)
> We need to hurry, but it is not worth driving recklessly. (to separate clauses in a compound sentence)
> When I see the list, however, I may

change my mind. (to set off transitional phrases)

The manager, Mr. Black, is away. (words in apposition)

The corner building, which used to house 40 people, is scheduled for demolition on Monday. (nonrestrictive phrase)

10,934 votes (in figures of 1,000 or more)

In some cases the comma should not, or at least need not, be used:

Post Office Box 7714 (with figures in an address)

He stood up and then he left. (to separate short clauses in a compound sentence)

After the war he worked in Los Angeles. (after a short introductory phrase)

The coat that has a button missing is fake fur. (to set off a restrictive clause)

The book *Sandcastles* is interesting. (to set off a restrictive appositive)

Dash. Too often the *dash* is used incorrectly or unnecessarily in place of a comma or colon. Sometimes it is incorrectly placed immediately after a colon. Used properly, a dash is intended to set off changes in thought, to set off a clause that summarizes a series, or to set off an appositional phrase that already contains commas:

John wrote an article—I think it was called "Forecast 2000"—about life in future decades.

The microphone was built in—or was it a separate mike?—on the last recorder we had.

Lettuce, carrots, stringbeans—these are all easy vegetables to grow.

I had the set—ring, bracelet, and necklace—delivered yesterday.

Ellipses. Dots or periods are used to show that words or sentences have been omitted. Occasionally secretaries use asterisks in place of dots, although a series of three or four periods is most common in printed material. Three dots are used to show words missing at the beginning or in the middle of a sentence. A fourth dot must be added to represent a period when the words (or sentences) are missing at the end of a sentence.

"The wheel had a serious defect . . . in workmanship."

". . . that is a new procedure in our company."

"Take it along when you leave town today. . . ."

Exclamation Point. People have a tendency not to use *exclamation marks* at all or to overuse them. Since this mark is used to emphasize something, it is no wonder that too many exclamation points on a page or in a paragraph have the opposite effect. There are so many that the reader loses any sense of surprise or emphasis. Here are some legitimate uses of the exclamation point:

Would you believe, it's July 1 and we're having a blizzard!
You look beautiful!
Great! Let's begin.
I can't imagine how he did it!
Winter Clearance Sale!

Hyphen. You should use the *hyphen* as follows: to divide words that must be carried over at the end of a line, to link two or more words serving as an adjective, to connect certain prefixes, to link words that are equal, to connect certain compound terms, to link numerator and denominator in fractions, to join a single letter to nouns or participles, and to indicate continuing or inclusive numbers:

> eva-sion
> well-organized cabinet
> two- and three-story houses
> ex-vice-president
> co-op
> Italian-American community
> mother-in-law
> one thousand and sixty-nine
> self-concept
> quasi-legal
> one-fifth
> X-ray
> 1980–81

Some words should not be hyphenated, however, for example, compound adjectives that contain adverbs ending in *ly,* compound adjectives that follow a noun, and prefixes and suffixes:

> happily married couple
> The cabinet is well organized.
> reestablish
> businesslike (but bell-like)

Leaders. These are a row of dots (periods) used to lead a reader's eye across a space. *Leaders* are most common in tables, statements, indexes, tables of content, and other forms of tabulation. Some secretaries use the hyphen key to make leaders, although the period is more familiar in most types of copy:

Chapter 9: Summary 214
Professional Services $325.00
Shipments overseas 1,242,000

Even though leaders are common, not everyone likes to see pages filled with dots or hyphens. Since they are usually not essential, anyone who objects to their appearance should simply omit them.

Parentheses. Like brackets, *parentheses* are used to enclose material that is not part of the general sentence structure. These marks are also used to enclose numbers or letters used with items in a series. Although parentheses are frequently helpful and have many proper uses, they should not be overused. Material enclosed in parentheses (or brackets) tends to slow the reading process and can adversely affect a reader's comprehension. When you do use these marks, however, be certain to keep punctuation that belongs with the parenthetical material *in-*

side the parentheses. In turn, punctuation that belongs to the main sentence should be *outside* the parentheses.

The following are examples of first-class matter: (1) letters, (2) postcards, (3) invoices, and (4) business reply mail.

One hundred dollars ($100)

Contemporary style books (e.g., *A Manual of Style*) show a trend toward lowercase letters.

The term is now obsolete (see *Webster's New Collegiate Dictionary*).

If you ask me (but I doubt that you will), it is time we concluded negotiations.

Period. The *period* is so familiar to everyone that most of its uses are well known and handled properly. The most common use is to end a declarative or imperative sentence. Other places where the period is used correctly are in abbreviations, after initials, following the numbers introducing lists, and as decimal points in numbers. Also, as described earlier, periods are used to make leaders in tabular matter and ellipses to show missing words and sentences.

This is a declarative sentence.

Write an imperative sentence.
C.O.D.
Calif.
R. T. Baxter
$19.52
6.8 percent

The following points were covered in her talk:

1. Setting objectives
2. Establishing priorities
3. Controlling interruptions

Do not use a period after initials of agencies, contractions, common short forms of words, or Roman numerals except in lists:

GAO (General Accounting Office)
ass'n (association)
memo (memorandum)
Henry VIII

Question Mark. Sometimes called the interrogation point, the *question mark* is used to conclude a direct question or express doubt. The placement of a question mark often depends on the type of interrogative phrase, as you can see from the following examples:

May I help you? (But: She asked if I needed help. Will you please help me with this.)

The campaign lasted three (?) years.

Does he do (a) ghostwriting or (b) by-line writing?

Does he do ghostwriting? by-line writing?

Quotation Marks. When you are using someone else's exact words, enclose the quoted material in *quotation marks*. Single quotation marks are used to enclose a quotation within a quotation. Quotation marks are also used to enclose the titles of articles, television programs, radio shows, songs, titles of unpublished works such as a thesis, short poems, chapters within a book, and nicknames. Quotes should not be used when material is set off as an extract, apart from the rest of the text, except for a quote within the extract. Neither should quotes be used in material set up in question-answer format. Familiar expressions (e.g., slang) are not enclosed in quotes either.

"Now," he said, "it is my pleasure to introduce our guest speaker."

"Anthony was right," she said, "when he acknowledged, 'Peace has come.' "

"Charlie's Angels"

"Star Spangled Banner"

"A Poem for You"

Chapter 9 is called "Urban Renewal"; the title is well suited to the discussion.

William "Wild Bill" Smith

Remember to place colons and semicolons *outside* the quotation marks; periods or commas always go on the *inside*.

Semicolon. One of the more interesting marks of punctuation, the *semicolon* can be used to break the monotony of a strict sentence-period style of writing. Similarly, it can be used to vary a comma-conjunction pattern. Other common applications of the semicolon are to separate items that already contain commas and to precede an adverb used as a conjunction:

It isn't for me to decide; how I wish that it were.

We need to make connections in Chicago; nevertheless, an earlier flight is out of the question.

The dealer offers storekeeper files, perma-snap files, and pull-drawer files; inventory schedules, retention schedules, and document-control schedules; and audit reports, audit work papers, and internal audit forms.

LEARNING CORRECT SPELLING AND WORD DIVISION

Spelling comes easy for some persons but not for others. The safest thing to do if you have any doubts about how to spell something is to look it up in your dictionary. A good dictionary is indispensable to a busy secretary. Even if you have a large, unabridged volume in your office, keep a smaller version on your desk at all times. *Webster's New Collegiate Dictionary* is an excellent desk-size dictionary based on the larger unabridged edition, *Webster's Third New International Dictionary.* Your dictionary should serve not only as a guide to correct spelling but also to correct pronunciation and syllabic division. In *Webster's,* for instance, a centered period shows the places where it is acceptable to divide a word at the end of a line. The following topics explain (1) spelling rules for the most common situations, such as plurals of compound terms, suffixes, prefixes, and words ending in *ie;* (2) rules for dividing words, that is, end-of-line division; and (3) troublesome words.

Basic Spelling Rules. Forming plurals is easier when you remember some of the most common rules. Most *abbreviations* are made plural, for example, by adding *s* (*depts.*); a few are made plural by doubling the singular letter (*pp.* for *pages*). *Figures and letters* are made plural by adding *'s* (*p's* and *q's*), unless the apostrophe is not needed for clarity (1980s). One of the most familiar rules states simply that the plural of words is usually formed by adding *s* alone (*hats*). Exceptions include words ending in *y* that are preceded by a consonant, where the *y* is then changed to *i* and *es* is added (*strawberries*). Some words ending in *f* or *fe* become *v*, adding *s* or *es* (*half* becomes *halves*). Words ending in *o* preceded by a consonant take an *es* (*tomatoes*). Compound terms usually have an *s* added to the most important word (*sisters-in-law*). Compound nouns are treated like other words adding *s* (*cupfuls*).

Suffixes are word endings such as *-able* and *-ment.* Those beginning with a vowel (*-age*) usually drop the word's final silent *e* (*use, usage*); those beginning with a consonant (*-ment*) usually keep the word's final silent *e* (*manage, management*) unless another vowel precedes the final *e* (*argue, argument*). Words that end in *y* preceded by a consonant change the *y* to *i* (*happy, happiest*) unless the suffix also begins with *i* (*fly, flying*); keep the *y* if it is preceded by a vowel (*enjoy, enjoyment*). Many of you may remember the rhyme Use *i* before *e* except after *c* or when sounded like *a* as in *neighbor* and *weigh* (*shield, receive, eight*).

When words ending in a silent *e* are preceded by *c* or *g*, they keep the final *e* before *-able* and *-ous* (*knowledgeable*). Use *-able* with most words ending in *-ation* (*adaptation, adaptable*). Because there is no general rule for words ending in *-ance* and *ence*, you should consult your dictionary when you are in doubt. Similarly, there is no rule applicable to the use of *-ise* and *-ize*. Only one word in English ends in *-sede*: supersede. Three end in *-ceed*: exceed, proceed, and succeed. All others take the ending *-cede* (*concede*).

Prefixes are word beginnings such as *dis-* and *non-*. Most words with a prefix should not be hyphenated (*antisocial*; but *anti-American*). *Self-*, however, takes a hyphen (*self-educated*; but *selfsame, oneself*). When a prefix is added to a word beginning with *s*, keep the *s* in the prefix, too (*dissatisfy*). Sometimes a prefix must be hyphenated for clarity (*re-form* means "to form again"; *reform* means "to remove faults").

Rules for Dividing Words. It is usually better not to divide words at the end of a line, but if you must, try to observe the basic rules for word division (check your dictionary when in doubt). Abbreviations however, should never be divided. Numbers should not be divided unless absolutely necessary; then divide them by one of the commas. Dates should be divided only between the day and the year. Proper names should not be divided at all, nor should the initials in a name be separated. Also avoid separating *Jr., Sr., II,* and *III* from the rest of a name. Other words that should not be divided are contractions (*didn't*), one-syllable words (*skilled*), and any word that has fewer than six letters (*usage*).

The place to divide a word is between syllables. Although dictionaries show all of the syllables, do not separate a one-letter syllable at the beginning or end of a word and try not to separate the first or last two letters from the rest of the word (not *grant-ed* or *a-round*). But when a one-letter syllable appears within a word, you should divide the word *after* that letter (*sepa-rate*) except with *-able* or *-ible* (*ad-miss-ible*). When there are two separate vowels together, divide the word between them (*recre-ation*). Also divide between two consonants that appear before a suffix (*occur-ring*). Compound words divide logically (*time-table*), and hyphenated words are logically separated at one of the hyphens (*father-in-law*).

Troublesome Words. However helpful general rules may be, there are always exceptions and unusual cases to present problems. Independent study, practice, and frequent usage will help you overcome many problems in spelling and word division. Numerous references and guides, in addition to your dictionary, are available to aid you in such efforts. For example, Dictation Disc Company (240 Madison Avenue, New York, NY 10016) has a list of 500 problem words, and secretarial and style books often refer to troublesome situations. Here are a few examples of words that are often misspelled:

accommodate
acknowledgment
acquiesce
advantageous
calendar
changeable
dilemma
existence
hypocrisy
intercede

judgment
negligible
occurrence
perseverance
practically
relevant
seize
supersede
supervisor
transferred

MASTERING THE BASIC RULES OF CAPITALIZATION

What should and should not be capitalized is a subject for debate among authorities. It is easier to point to trends, for example, more lowercase letters, than to outline firm rules and principles of capitalization. Frequently organizations, book publishers, magazines, and newspapers have their own preferred house style. Specialized fields of study, such as psychology, often adopt a certain set of rules and principles that differ from those characteristic of other disciplines. How do you cope with such diversity, and how do you know who is right or wrong? The only sensible course is to use the style (if any) preferred by your organization or by the field of activity associated with your organization—and, particularly, to be consistent with whatever style you use. If you are unable to determine the required style where you work, you may observe the rules described in the following sections with confidence, since they are widely accepted among contemporary writers and publishers. The terms and references described below are abbreviations, educational references, geographical terms, governmental-political terms, historical terms, holidays and seasons, judiciary, legislation, military services, numbers, organizations, quotations, religious references, titles, and trade names.

Abbreviations. Most dictionaries indicate whether an abbreviation should be capitalized. One rule of thumb is that abbreviations are capitalized when the words they represent are also capitalized, but this rule is not strictly observed in the business world. Abbreviations for agencies, military units, and other organizations are always capitalized. Some academic degrees are capitalized, but others are uppercase and lowercase. Directions in streets are capitalized, and acronymns are capitalized as a rule unless they have become a familiar part of speech such as *laser*.

FBI
IBM
Col. Mary Collins, USA
2000 Columbus Circle, NW
Ph.D.
M.B.A.
OPEC
C.P.A.
TV

radar

Jan.

ft.

f.o.b.

p.m.

A list of common abbreviations is presented in the Guide to Miscellaneous Data. Keep in mind that most abbreviations (e.g., *ft.*) are not acceptable in general text or in correspondence. They are used more in informal note taking, in certain technical writing, and in footnotes, tables, and so forth.

Educational References. The formal names of schools and colleges and their departments should be capitalized. However, general references to a school or department are lowercased. Similarly, an official class name is capitalized but not a general reference to the class. Official academic degrees and honors are capitalized unless they are not part of a name or title. The formal title of a course of study is capitalized, but a general reference to a subject of study is lowercased, unless it is a proper name such as *English*.

New York   Central College
  University

Mount Wilson High School	B. R. Adams, Bachelor of Arts
Lewisville Junior High School	junior college
Rosemont Day Care Center	high school
	the university
Department of History	junior high
	science department
Junior Class	a freshman
Introductory Chemistry II	bachelor's degree
	the fellowship
Arthur Wright Fellowship	secretarial studies
	doctorate

Geographical Terms. Countries, continents, and regions are capitalized, but adjectival references to them are lowercased. Popular (not official) names for places are usually capitalized, too; a term such as *ghetto*, however, is lowercased. *Coast* is capitalized when reference is to a specific locality but lowercased when it is part of a geographic designation. General directions are not capitalized unless the reference is to a section of the United States.

West Germany	the South
Orient	Mississippi Valley
Middle East	South Shore
Western world	West Coast (U.S.)
North Hemisphere	Hudson River
Corn Belt	North Atlantic

English Channel	Maine coast
South Pole	northern Egypt
to the north	the equator
the valley	polar regions

Governmental-Political Terms. Formal political divisions such as states are capitalized unless they precede a name or stand alone. Names of organizations and movements are capitalized, too, but not words such as *party* or *movement*. General political descriptions that frequently end in *-ism* are not capitalized. Designations such as *federal* are capitalized if they are part of an official title; otherwise they are lowercased. The official names of bodies such as legislatures are capitalized, but general references to them are lowercased. Formal units such as a district are also capitalized, but general references to them are lowercased.

United Nations Security Council	Communist party
General Assembly of Illinois	Republicans
Iowa State	Forest County
Congress	Federal Aviation Agency
Madison City Council	San Francisco Board of Education
Department of Welfare	Reichstag
	the council

state of California
congressional
the department
the federal
  government

the legislature
the board
communism

Historical Terms. The numerical designations of periods and eras are lowercased
unless they are part of an official title.
Cultural periods, though, are usually capitalized. Documents of historical importance are capitalized, too, although a
general reference such as *war* is lowercased.

Middle Ages
World War I
Prohibition
Renaissance
Stone Age
Reign of Terror
New Deal
Declaration of
  Independence
Neolithic times
Victorian era
the war

the depression
colonial period
  (U.S.)
twentieth century
antiquity
space age
cold war
westward
  movement
gold rush
ancient Rome

Holidays and Seasons. Religious holidays and seasons and feast days are always
capitalized. Special days and secular holidays are also capitalized. However, a gen-

eral description such as *election day* is lowercased. The four seasons are lowercased, too, but days of the week and months of the year are capitalized. One exception is that when seasons are personified, they should always be capitalized.

Good Friday	March
April Fools' Day	inauguration day
Halloween	fall
Labor Day	winter solstice
Veterans Day	vernal equinox
Hanukkah	At last Winter
Ash Wednesday	cometh.
Thursday	

Judiciary. Full names of courts are capitalized. But the word *court* alone is usually lowercased, except when it refers to the presiding judge making a decision or when it refers to the United States Supreme Court. *Bar* and *bench* are capitalized only when they are part of an official name. Types of courts such as family court are lowercased.

United States Supreme Court	Nevada Supreme Court
Circuit Court of Hickory County	Municipal Court of Cincinnati

American Bar
  Association
New York Court
  of Appeals
the Court
  (U.S. Supreme)
District Court
  for the Northern
  District of
  Michigan
The Court
  sustained
  the motion.

the bar
juvenile court
county court
state supreme
  court
municipal court
court of appeals
traffic court

Legislation. Acts, treaties, bills, codes, laws, policies, and so on, are capitalized. Brief, general references to such legislative matters, however, are lowercased. A reference to pending legislation is also lowercased. The word *constitution* is capitalized only when it is part of the official title of a specific constitution. Amendments to the Constitution are capitalized only when you refer to them by number or full title.

Magna Charta
Wisconsin
  Constitution
Bill of Rights
Pact of Paris
Open Door Policy
Marshall Plan

Sixteenth
  Amendment
pending gun-
  control bill
the Constitution
  (U.S.)

the state   the plan
  constitution   due process clause
the doctrine   the amendment

Military Services. The formal names of
military services are capitalized, but general references such as *army* are lowercased. Branches and divisions of the
armed forces are also capitalized.

United States   Rough Riders
  Army   Coast Guard
United States   Signal Corps
  Signal Corps   the army
National Guard   the guard
Red Army   Russian army
Royal Air Force   British air force
First Battalion   the battalion
Fifth Army   the fleet
Luftwaffe   Allied forces
Pacific Fleet   the task force

Numbers. Capitalize numbers that are
part of a formal title and those that are
part of a street address (numbers 12 or below are spelled out in street addresses).
Sums of money mentioned in legal documents are capitalized, and often they are
capitalized in ordinary business correspondence. Numbers of specific political
and military divisions and units are also

capitalized, including certain dynasties and governments.

Fifth Precinct
First National Bank
Third Battalion
Sixth Ward
Twenty-fourth Regiment
Third Reich
Eightieth Congress
214 Second Avenue
One Park Avenue
his check for Ten Dollars ($10)

Organizations. The full, official names of companies, institutions, and associations should be capitalized. But lowercase the word *the* preceding a name in textual matter even if it is part of the official title. Lowercase general descriptive terms that are not part of the title. One exception to this rule is that a general descriptive name such as *corporation* is capitalized in legal documents when it stands for a specific organization.

League of Women Voters

New Jersey Humane Society

Follett Publishing Company

University of Illinois

Ford Motor Company	the company (in general copy)
Girl Scouts of America	the Corporation (in legal documents)
National Science Foundation	the union

Quotations. Writers often change the first letter of a quotation from all caps to lowercase or vice versa to fit their own passages. Frequently when a quotation is used as part of a writer's sentence, it begins with a lowercase letter. The first letter of an *extract* (a block quotation set apart from the rest of the text) may be lowercased, too, if desired. But any such changes of initial letters must be put in brackets in legal works.

> The postmaster said, "a $40 annual fee must be paid in advance."
> As the postmaster said: "A $40 annual fee must be paid in advance."
> "A $40 annual fee," said the postmaster, "must be paid in advance."

Religious References. Capitalize the names of deities; appellations of revered persons; full, formal names of religious groups and organizations; historic councils and meetings; and names of the Bible and its books and divisions. Lowercase *church* unless it is part of an official title. The current trend is also to lowercase pronouns referring to God unless capitalization is necessary to avoid ambiguity. Some words, called Platonic ideas, such as *truth,* may be capitalized when they are used in a religious context.

First Methodist
   Church of Troy
God
Allah
the Almighty
Talmud
Buddhism
Orthodoxy
Second Vatican
   Council
Holy Writ
the Gospels
the Sacrament
the Creation
Original Sin
a Gentile
Roman Catholic
Anglican
   communion
gentile laws
a high mass
vesper service
rosary

Titles. A general rule of thumb is to capitalize titles that precede a name but to lowercase them when they follow a name or stand alone. These are a few exceptions to this rule: Some British titles are capitalized when standing alone; honorific titles are always capitalized even when used alone; when certain fellowships and professorships are used with a name, they, too, are capitalized; fictitious names are usually capitalized; and the Speaker of the House is always capitalized, even when used alone, to avoid ambiguity.

President Jimmy Carter

Acting Secretary of State Daniels

Reverend Paul Sloane

the First Lady

Prince of Wales

Your Majesty

the Great Emancipator

John Doe

William Drew, Fellow of the Royal Academy

Today Headquarters called.

Noah Hill, professor of economics

the pope

the president

the chief justice of the United States

Elizabeth, queen of England

a Fulbright scholar

doctor's degree

the senator

the chairman of the department

the bishop of Manchester

Trade Names. Capitalize registered trademark names but lowercase a general reference to a product associated with the formal name.

Coca-Cola	soft drink
Levi's	blue jeans
Kleenex	tissue

Chapter 9
Using Current Letter-Writing Practices

Letter-writing practices have changed significantly in the past decade, particularly in tone (more casual, more friendly) and in the increasing use of the memo in external as well as internal communications. Many secretaries are expected not only to correct and polish their employers' correspondence but also to compose routine letters and memos for their own signatures. Written contacts, inside and outside, are vital to the successful functioning of the office—to the entire organization, in fact. The impression created by a letter or memo—its neatness, accuracy, clarity, attitude, and so on—can promote or discourage a positive response. The area of written communication is one in which a secretary can be a great asset to her employer and can make a substantial contribution to the organization.

SETTING UP THE LETTER

Before you can write effective letters, you need to know how to set them up: how to arrange and treat the principal elements, such as the dateline, and what style or layout to use. Your employer probably has a preference in these matters. If the preferred treatment is not obvious from file copies of correspondence in your office, you should ask if a particular style is required. In any case, you may have to make some choices yourself, and the following sections are intended to give you the information you need to make such decisions. The principal elements described below are the attention line, blind carbon-copy notation, body, carbon-copy notation, complimentary close, dateline, enclosure notation, envelope, identification line, inside address, mail-instruction placement, personal notation, postscript, reference line, salutation, second-page heading, signature, and subject line. (For a description of the principal elements of the memo, see Selecting Letter and Memo Formats, page 217.)

Attention Line. Some letters are addressed to a firm but are directed to the attention of a specific individual. This procedure indicates that the letter is not personal and may be opened by someone else if the individual is not there. An *attention line* must appear on both the letter and the envelope. On the envelope the line is typed two spaces below the last line of the address and slightly to the left. On the letterhead it is typed two spaces below the inside address (and two spaces above the salutation). The salutation on such a letter would be *Gentlemen,* since the letter would be addressed to the firm. If the firm is composed of women, the salutation would be *Ladies* or *Mesdames.* For firms composed of both men and women, use *Ladies and Gentlemen.* Although the preferred attention line gives the full name of an individual, it is permissible to use a last name only or even to use a job title alone.

Attention Mrs. Helen Benjamin
Attention Mrs. Benjamin
Attention Credit Manager

Blind Carbon-Copy Notation. You may at times need to send a carbon copy of correspondence to someone without the addressee knowing about it. In such case you would omit the traditional carbon-copy notation (c.c. Ms. Norris) on the original and instead type a *blind notation* (b.c. Ms. Norris) on the carbon copy only. Remove the original, any other copies, and the carbon sheets and type the notation about one inch from the top at the left margin. The following are common forms for this notation (with or without the periods):

b.c. Mr. Lewis
b.c.c. Mrs. Jones

Body. Single-space all but very short letters, with a double space between paragraphs. Indent paragraphs five to ten spaces (except with the block and simplified formats, which are set flush left). The overall position of the *body* of a letter on the page is determined by the number of words in the letter. Many secretaries mark up sample letters (copied from letters in the files) by word count and use such samples as guides in positioning short letters (less than one hundred words), medium-sized letters (one hundred to two hundred words) and long letters (more than two hundred words). Such samples should include other factors that affect length: attention lines, subject lines, lists, and so on. To save time, some secretaries make adjustments only at the top and bottom of the letter; others compensate for length variations by moving margins in and out as well. Use the method preferred in your office (if any) or the one that works best for you in seeing that letters of all sizes are positioned attractively on the page. (The different layouts in use today are described later in this chapter.)

Carbon-Copy Notation. Unlike the blind notation, the *carbon-copy notation* is typed on the original and any other copies for the recipients to see. This notation is often the last thing typed on a letter—except for a postscript, which is always typed below everything else. It is positioned flush left, two spaces beneath any other notation above it. The following are examples of acceptable forms of the carbon-copy notation:

> cc: H.A. Baker
> c.c. Ms. Foster
> Copy to Miss R. S. Comstocke

Complimentary Close. The position of the *complimentary close* depends on the letter format you use (see Selecting Letter and Memo Formats, p. 217). In the block letter style, for example, the complimentary close is typed flush left. With some of the other popular formats, it is typed slightly to the right of center page. In all cases it is typed two spaces below the body of the letter. The first word is capitalized and, with standard punctuation, a comma follows the last word. If the letter runs onto a second page, keep at least two lines from the continued body on the second page before the closing. The trend today is to use an informal, friendly closing such as the following (but for dignitaries and high officials use *Respectfully yours* or *Very truly yours*):

Sincerely	Regards
Sincerely yours	Best regards
Cordially	Best wishes
Cordially yours	All the best

Dateline. Depending on the letter format you use, the *dateline* is typed either flush left or flush right. Usually it is typed 2 to 4 spaces below the letterhead, but this position may be adjusted for different size letters. The space between the dateline and the first line of the inside address also may be adjusted from 2 to 12 spaces. Most business and professional writers use the month-day-year (April 5, 1980) style for the dateline. But some organizations (e.g., the military) omit the comma and place the day first (5 April 1980). Only formal invitations spell out the day or year.

Shortened or abbreviated forms (4-5-80) are not used in traditional business correspondence. Datelines should show the day a letter is dictated, not the day it is typed.

Enclosure Notation. When you enclose something with your letter, you should type an *enclosure notation* at the bottom two lines below the dictator and typist's reference initials against the left margin. (Some secretaries also use this position to indicate that an item was sent separately rather than enclosed.) These are examples of common enclosure notations:

Enc.
Enclosure
2 Encs.
Enc. 2
Enc. Form 623 (to be returned)
Enc. Ck. no. 1180, $260
Enclosures: Check
             Policy 44-2211-09-X
             Policy 126-0041-22-M

Envelope. The address on an *envelope* should be the same as the inside address of the letter. It is most often typed single-spaced in block style slightly to the left and below the center of the envelope. The organization's name and return address is usually printed in the upper left corner.

The name of the writer may be typed above the organization's printed name if desired. The mailing address—and preferably the return address, too—should comply with current postal standards. This means using zip codes with all addresses. The U.S. Postal Serice also recommends using their official two-letter state abbreviations (see Guide to Miscellaneous Data). Acceptable positions for notations and directions sometimes vary with writers, but usually attention lines are typed below the address and to the left; *Personal* and *Confidential* notations are often typed above the address and slightly to the left; delivery notations such as *Special Delivery* are commonly typed to the right under the postage stamp or meter imprint.

Identification Line. Reference initials on a letter show who dictated it and who typed it. Organizations handle these *identification lines* differently. Some want both dictator and typist's initials on the original and every copy; others do not require the dictator's initials if the dictator is also the person who signs the letter; still others want the initials only on the office file copy; and some organizations require a third set of initials if one person dictates the letter, another types it, and someone else signs it. The correct place for reference initials is flush left across from or two spaces below the signature line, except with the official style of letter where the initials are placed two spaces below the address. These are acceptable identification lines:

jv
MRC:jv
MRC:TP:jv
M. R. Clark:jv

Inside Address. The *inside address* is typed flush left 2 to 12 spaces below the dateline, except with an official style of letter, where it is placed 2 spaces beneath the signature line against the left margin. Carry-over lines should be indented about 3 spaces. Job titles may be omitted if the address runs over four lines. Company names should be typed according to their official listing. Post office box numbers are preferred over street addresses, if there is a choice. Although streets, job titles, and so on should not be abbreviated, the U.S. Postal Service prefers that you use two-letter state abbreviations (see Guide to Miscellaneous Data) followed by the zip code. Keep the city and state on the same line. (For further details on personal titles such as *Ms.* see Using the Correct Forms of Address, page 222.)

Mail-Instruction Placement. In case a letter needs to be traced later, some organizations want the mailing notation that goes on the envelope to be typed on the file copy of the letter as well. Usually notations such as *Special Delivery* are positioned flush left two lines below the dateline or two lines beneath the enclosure notation. They may be typed in all capital letters or in uppercase and lowercase and underscored.

Personal Notation. The *personal notations* that are placed on an envelope (e.g., *Confidential*) should also be typed on the original and the file copy. This type of notation is usually typed flush left four spaces above the inside address. Frequently it is typed in caps and lowercase and underscored. Use *Confidential* and *Personal* notations only when the addressee alone is expected to open the letter, but do not use these notations as a device to catch the addressee's attention.

Postscript. Some persons object to *postscripts,* believing that all thoughts should be incorporated in the body of the letter, not tacked on as an afterthought at the end. But many other writers believe that using a postscript is a legitimate way to add a thought to a letter that is already prepared or to emphasize a thought that might otherwise receive less attention in the body of the letter. A first postscript (P.S.) is typed beneath the last item at the bottom of the letter; a second postscript (P.P.S.) is typed beneath the first one. Use the same paragraph indentation you use in the body of the letter when you type the postscript(s).

Reference Line. Companies that use numerical files often include a numerical *reference notation* on all correspondence— file numbers, order numbers, and so on (e.g., In reference to: Our order 00311G). If you receive correspondence with a reference notation, be certain to include the number on your own letter when you reply (e.g., Your reference no. 7010). Many company letterheads have words such as *In reference to* or *In reply please refer to* already printed at the top of the page. The typist then merely types in the correct number. If nothing is preprinted, however, type the full line two to four spaces directly beneath the dateline.

Salutation. The *salutation* is typed flush left two spaces below the inside address. In traditional business letters the salutation is followed by a colon. In social and personal correspondence a comma is frequently used. Capitalize the first word (Dear), the title (Mrs.), and the addressee's name. The trend today is to use a friendly, informal salutation (Dear Harry) among associates. Otherwise you should use *Mr.,* *Mrs., Miss,* or *Ms.,* and if the person has a title such as *Dr.* or *Colonel* or *Reverend,* you should use the appropriate title (Dear Dr. Jones). Ask if you have any doubts about the way your employer prefers to address someone. (Further information is given in Using the Correct Forms of Address, page 222. Also see the Guide to Miscellaneous Data for a listing of correct forms of address for dignitaries.)

Second-Page Heading. *Continued pages* may have preprinted headings but are frequently blank sheets of paper comparable to the letterhead paper stock. Carry at least two lines over to the second page and keep at least two lines of a new paragraph at the bottom of the first page. (Do not type *continued* at the bottom of the first page.) The heading of the second page should have the addressee's name, the page number, and the date. Begin about one or one and one-half inches from the top and leave two or three lines between the head and the continued body of the letter. Either of the following headings is acceptable on continued pages:

Miss Jan Fox   2   July 9, 19—

Miss Jan Fox
Page 2
July 9, 19—

Signature. The signer's name is usually typed four spaces directly beneath the complimentary close. Some *signature lines* consist of the signer's name and job title. Others use only the person's name or only the person's job title. Certain types of businesses (e.g., accounting firms) require individuals to sign letters for the firm. Signature lines in this case often consist of the firm name typed two spaces below the complimentary close and the signer's name four spaces beneath the firm name. There may also be slight variations of the above arrangements. When you sign a letter for your employer, writing his or her name, place your initials directly below the signature you write. But if you sign the letter in your own name, type *Secretary to*

Mr./Mrs./Miss/Ms. X for the signature line and write your own full name directly above it. Signature lines are typed in uppercase and lowercase letters. For example:

> With job title:
> Donald J. Mackenzie
> President
> (to be signed *Donald J. Mackenzie*)

> Using given name:
> (Mrs.) Joan Franklin
> (to be signed *Joan Franklin*)

> Using married name:
> (Mrs. Thomas K. Franklin)
> (to be signed *Joan Franklin*)

> Unmarried woman:
> (Miss) Lois Welsh or Lois Welsh
> (to be signed *Lois Welsh*)

> Note: An unmarried woman should not use *Ms.* in her signature.

> Secretary signs her own name:
> Secretary to Mr. Mackenzie
> (to be signed *Ella R. Carlson*)

> Using firm name with dictator's name and title:
> Fosdick Industries

Paul J. LeBlond
Branch Manager
(to be signed *Paul J. LeBlond*)

Subject Line. Writers use a *subject line* to identify the subject of the letter. The reader can see instantly then what the letter is about without reading through it. Type the subject line two spaces *below* the salutation either centered or flush left depending on your letter format. Double-space again to the first line of the body of the letter. These are a few common styles for a subject line:

Subject: Open House
SUBJECT: OPEN HOUSE
<u>Subject: Open House</u>
<u>Subject</u>: Open House
Subject: <u>Open House</u>
Re: Open House

SELECTING LETTER AND MEMO FORMATS

Your office probably has a preferred letter style, although the selection is often left to the secretary. There are several basic letter styles to choose from, yet at least 90 percent of all letters are typed in a block format. The style you use should enhance the overall appearance and impact of your letter. The letterhead, the care you exercise in typing the letter, the tone of its contents—all contribute to the impact. Five basic styles are described below, along with a summary of the principal features common to the memo format.

Full-Block Letter. One of the easiest letters to type is the *full-block style*. Everything is set flush left so you do not have to indent paragraphs or set tab stops for the dateline and closing lines. Open punctuation may be used with this style to increase the ease of typing. This would mean no colon after the salutation or comma after the complimentary close and no comma between the city and two-letter state abbreviation in the inside address. Because everything is aligned at the left, the full-block letter has a neat, modern look preferred by many writers.

Block Letter. The *block format* is probably more popular than anything else because it retains many of the timesaving features of the flush-left, full-block style but breaks up the rigid left margin by positioning the dateline and reference line flush right and the complimentary close and signature lines just slightly right of the center of the page. But as in the full-block style, paragraphs and everything else here are flush left, too. As another timesaving feature, you also may use open punctuation with this style, although many writers prefer standard punctuation (e.g., comma after the complimentary close, colon after the salutation, and comma between city and state in the address.)

Semiblock Letter. Traditionalists usually prefer a *semiblock letter* format. This style has a somewhat softer look as each paragraph is indented five to ten spaces. Dateline and reference line are flush right, and the complimentary close and signature lines are typed slightly right of center page. Standard punctuation is common with the semiblock letter. Setup time may be slightly longer with this format because several elements must be positioned to the right and each paragraph must be indented. But proponents believe the time involved is minimal and, in any case, the pleasing appearance is worth the extra effort.

Official Style. There are times when a *formal,* or *personal, style* is needed. Your employer may, for example, use this style for personal letters written on smaller monarch-sized stationery. With this format the inside address is typed flush left two to five spaces *below* the signature line. The dateline is flush right, and the complimentary close and signature lines are typed slightly to the right of center page. Paragraphs are indented five to ten spaces. Thus this letter resembles the semiblock letter except for the position of the inside address. Punctuation is usually standard, though the comma may be omitted between the city and two-letter state abbreviation in the address.

Simplified Style. The *simplified letter style* is less common than some of the others, but organizations using it are particularly impressed with its modern appearance and timesaving features. All elements including paragraphs are positioned flush left as they are in the full-block format, and open punctuation is common. But there is no salutation and no complimentary close. Instead writers begin the body of the letter with an informal remark, for example, "Thank you, Mr. Brown, for letting us know that your report will be in the mail this week." This opening sentence is typed two spaces below the inside address. Similarly the last sentence of the body takes the place of the traditional closing: "We sincerely appreciate your help on this important project." The traditional signature lines, then, are placed about four spaces beneath this final line of the body of the letter.

The Memo. Organizations are using the *memo format* more and more, even in external communications. It is easy to set up and can be typed on less expensive, preprinted memo stationery—sometimes with a place for the recipient to reply on the same sheet or on an attached duplicate copy. Memo headings are typically typed in after preprinted words such as: *Date, To, Dept., From,* and *Subject* or *Re.* Each office has a preferred heading, and frequently the secretary selects memo forms from the standard styles offered by manufacturers. The body of a memo begins two lines down from the heading and is often blocked with a line between each paragraph. Like letters, memos are single-spaced unless they are extremely short. Notations (e.g., enclosures) are handled the same as with a letter format. But there is no complimentary close and often no signature line, though many preprinted forms have a ruled line at the bottom for signatures. Internal memos are sent in special reusable company envelopes; external memos are sent in a regular mailing envelope addressed as if a regular letter were enclosed.

USING THE CORRECT FORMS OF ADDRESS

Secretaries need to be sensitive to the subtle changes that are continually taking place in the business world. Examples of changing times are evident in contemporary forms of address, particularly in the correct use of personal titles. Most secretaries realize it is important to remember names and to pronounce and spell them correctly. This same degree of concern should be applied in using the correct forms of address. For example, a professional person who has earned a Ph.D. degree usually wants to be addressed with the title *Dr.* To help you exercise care in such matters, the following sections describe current trends in using (1) personal titles, (2) professional titles, and (3) honorific titles. (See the Guide to Miscellaneous Data for a list of abbreviated titles and degrees and a list of correct forms of address for dignitaries.)

Personal Titles. When a man or woman has no professional title such as

Dr., you should use *Mr., Mrs., Miss,* or *Ms.* These personal titles are used before a name in the inside address, in the salutation, and in any references to the addressee in the body of the letter. Such titles are used even when a job title follows a name (Mrs. Eva Marx, President). However, a personal title is *not* used when *Esquire* follows a name (Norman Hill, Esquire). When you do not know the marital status of a woman, use *Ms.* Some women prefer this title anyway. Otherwise a woman's name is preceded by *Miss* or *Mrs.* In business a married or widowed woman may be addressed by her husband's name (Mrs. Jeffrey Kingston) or by her given name (Mrs. Paula Kingston). A divorced woman in business may use *Mrs., Miss,* or *Ms.* with her maiden name (Ms. Ellen Osmon) or *Mrs.* with her given and married names (Mrs. Ellen Sims). Use the form the addressee prefers if you know it.

Professional Titles. When a person has a professional title such as *Dr., Mayor, Colonel, Professor,* or *Reverend,* be certain to use that title (Professor Lloyd Rhome). In most cases, you should address a woman with a professional title by her given and married names (Dr. Jeanne Fry; Drs. Henry and Jeanne Fry; Dr. Jeanne

Fry and Mr. Henry Fry). When degrees are placed after a name, use only the highest degree, or if both are equivalent, place the one pertaining to the person's occupation first (for a professor of philosophy: Lloyd Rhome, Ph.D., Sc.D.). But do not use a title before the name and degrees after it (*not* Professor Lloyd Rhome, Ph.D., Sc.D.).

Honorific Titles. Dignitaries and other persons with official or honorary positions should be addressed with their official title, even after retirement in many instances (General Warren Gregg, U.S.A., Retired; The Honorable Rosalind Damon). A listing in the Guide to Miscellaneous Data shows how to handle honorific titles in the inside address and salutation. As a general rule women are addressed the same as men except, of course, that *Madam* is used instead of *Sir* in salutations.

COMPOSING LETTERS AND MEMOS

Every letter and memo you write represents your employer. To create the best possible impression, your correspondence must be typed neatly and accurately, with proper punctuation and capitalization. It must have all the structural elements positioned in the proper places according to the format you choose. Special care must be taken to address the recipient correctly. Each piece needs to be examined for grammatical accuracy and for any evidence of trite terms and ambiguous phrases. The tone throughout should be friendly and cooperative. In short, your correspondence must encompass all the essentials of good writing that together create the right impression in the right way at the right time. This section describes (1) the type of writing you do for your own and other signatures, (2) when to use a letter format and when to use a memo format, and (3) how to improve your skills in composition.

Writing for Your Own and Other Signatures. Since secretarial duties in general vary widely from one position to another, it is to be expected that letter-writing responsibilities will vary, too. Some secretaries routinely correct and type correspondence dictated by others but do not compose anything on their own; others occasionally draft routine letters for their employers' signatures as well as some for their own signature. Although there is no firm rule, some examples of letters written by secretaries for their own signature are routine inquiries, orders, reminders and follow-ups, adjustments pertaining to accounts and billing problems, reservations, appointment letters, and acknowledgments. Examples of correspondence composed by secretaries for their employers to sign are letters of acceptance or regret, appreciation, congratulations, sympathy, introduction, holiday greetings, and so forth.

Whether to Use a Letter or Memo. Traditionally the guideline concerning letters and memos has been that memos are a form of *internal* communication primarily intended to convey objective, factual information, and letters have been regarded as the correct *external* communication tool for any purpose—to express good wishes as well as to convey factual data. In the past decade, however, this distinction has become blurred. Letters are still used externally, and memos are still used internally, of course, but many firms now use the less formal, less expensive, and easier-to-set-up memo (and speed message) format for certain external correspondence: routine inquiries and orders, transmittal notes, brief confirmations, and informal contacts with business acquaintances and longtime customers. Follow the practice in your office if you have any doubts.

Improving Your Skills in Composition. Skilled letter writers use a natural, conversational tone in business correspondence. They never use a large word (*utilization*) when a small one (*use*) will do as well. The same goes for sentences—the shorter the better in most cases. Good writers avoid unnecessary words or phrases (attached *hereto*) and do not use two words that mean the same thing (*first and foremost*). Similarly, they never use stilted language (*Replying to your kind favor of*) or a discourteous or an unfriendly tone (*You made a mistake, which we expect you to rectify immediately*). Some words tend to antagonize (*mistake, unsatisfactory, failure,* and so on) and thus should be avoided. Skilled writers always take a positive approach (*We will fill your order promptly upon receipt of your check for $12.98,* not *We cannot fill your order until we receive your check for $12.98*). Finally, good writers use friendly openings that get right to the point, using the recipient's name if possible (*We appreciate your interest in our ovenware, Mrs. Arnold*). Endings, too, should close on a friendly note (*We hope* *you enjoy this lovely ovenware set for many years to come).*

MODEL LETTERS AND MEMOS

Eighteen sample letters and memos are shown below, including a formal invitation and a formal acceptance. These are examples of communications frequently prepared by a secretary for her own or someone else's signature: acknowledgment, apology, appointment, appreciation, collection, complaint, confirmation, follow-up, introduction, informal invitation and reply, formal invitation and reply, order, request, reservation, sympathy, and thank you.

Acknowledgment

Dear Ms. Porter:

Your letter to Mr. Halsted concerning the new marketing schedule has arrived during his temporary absence from the office. However, I know he'll be very pleased to find the schedule on his desk when he returns, and I'm certain he'll contact you promptly at that time.

If I can be of any help in the meantime, please do let me know.

Sincerely,

Apology

Dear Mr. Madison:

We're very sorry for the delay in delivering your February 25 order. It was shipped by REA Express on May 3 but was returned to us on May 7 because of an insufficient address. We corrected the address and shipped the order again on May 9, so it should reach you within a few days.

Please accept our apologies for any inconvenience the delay has caused. We appreciate your patience.

Cordially yours,

Appointment

Dear Mr. Lewis:

Mr. Newcombe will be happy to see you during your trip to San Francisco and would like to know if you can come to his office at two o'clock on Friday, October 4.

Please let me know whether this time will be convenient for you. Thank you very much.

Sincerely,

Appreciation

Dear Jan:

I sincerely appreciated your help in organizing the Wednesday workshops at our spring seminar. We couldn't have managed without your able assistance. But thanks to the superb job by you and your committee, the program was a huge success.

Hope we can work together soon again, Jan.

Best regards,

Collection

Dear Mr. Hendricks:

Just a friendly reminder that your account of $21.99 is past due.

If your check is already in the mail, please disregard this notice and accept our thanks. Otherwise, your prompt payment will be very much appreciated.

Sincerely yours,

Complaint

Gentlemen:

Your May 30 statement no. 07166G shows a charge of $53 for 5,000 note pads. This is the third statement we have received, although the order was canceled on February 1 and the note pads were therefore never sent.

A copy of our letter of cancellation is enclosed for your reference. We would appreciate it if you would correct your records accordingly and send us confirmation of our cancellation. Thank you.

Sincerely yours,

Confirmation

Dear Linda:

Yes, I'm still planning to attend the executive committee's 7:30 p.m. dinner meeting on Friday, July 14, at the Boatmen's Inn.

Thanks very much for reminding me.

Cordially,

Follow-up

TO: Barry Wendall

FROM: Marcia Cross

RE: Conference Papers

Just a brief reminder that the paper you're preparing
for our conference proceedings is due February 28.
In the meantime, I'd appreciate it if you would drop
me a note indicating (1) estimated length in typed,
double-spaced pages and (2) number of anticipated
illustrations.

Thanks, Barry.

Introduction

Dear Jim:

It's my pleasure to introduce to you Mr. John
Lawrence of Addison Manufacturing Company, who is
visiting Minneapolis to explore the possibilities
of establishing a branch office in that location.

I know that any advice you can give Mr. Lawrence
would be most welcome. I'm certain he would also
find it very helpful if you could introduce him to
other business people around Minneapolis who might
be able to offer additional information on the
prospects for his company in your area.

Thanks very much, Jim.

Regards,

Invitation—Informal

Dear Jackie:

Would you be free to have lunch with me and Fred Wright on Tuesday, December 5, at 12 noon? I'd like to have you both be my guests at the Seafarer Restaurant.

Let me know if you can come. Fred and I are looking forward to hearing more about your new West Coast Division.

Best wishes,

Invitation—Informal Reply

Dear Sam:

I'd be delighted to join you and Fred for lunch at the Seafarer Restaurant on Tuesday, December 5, at 12 noon.

Many thanks for asking.

Cordially,

Invitation—Formal

Mr. and Mrs. Dale Penella
request the pleasure of
Mr. and Mrs. Johnson's
company at dinner
on Wednesday, the fourth of October
at eight o'clock
Seventeen West Boulevard

Black tie
R.S.V.P.

Invitation—Formal Reply

Mr. and Mrs. Kenneth Johnson
accept with pleasure
the kind invitation of
Mr. and Mrs. Penella
to be present at dinner
on Wednesday, the fourth of October
at eight o'clock
at Seventeen West Boulevard

Order

TO: Office Suppliers, Inc.

FROM: Jane Montgomery
      Office Manager

SUBJECT: Expansion Envelopes

Please send us the following:

    100, 12" x 10" x 2", no. S-1-810

    Printed Expansion Envelopes, $34.95

We would like to have four lines imprinted for our
return address:

    Special Services Department
    Kraft Appliance Manufacturers, Inc.
    Post Office Box 61901
    Dallas, Texas 75262

Please send the invoice and shipment to my attention
at Kraft Appliance Manufacturers. Thank you.

Request

Dear Ted:

I've heard so many fine things about your new conveyor system that I was wondering if you would be willing to explain its operation to our field staff. It helps them communicate with our customers more knowledgeably and effectively when they understand the functioning of such systems in our company.

We're having a staff meeting next Thursday, August 21, at 9:30 a.m. Would you be able to attend and share your ideas with us then for about 10 to 15 minutes?

Thanks, Ted. I hope you'll be able to come.

Regards,

Reservation

Gentlemen:

Please reserve first-class space for Mrs. Carmen Munson, director of research, Atlantis Institute, on your flight number 140 out of Cincinnati to San Francisco on Monday, September 9, at 9:30 a.m., central standard time. Mrs. Munson would like to return from San Francisco to Cincinnati on your flight number 611, Wednesday, September 11, at 11:40 a.m., Pacific standard time.

The ticket should be charged to Atlantis Institute's air travel account Z1003264Y. Mrs. Munson will pick up her ticket at the terminal just before departure.

Please confirm this reservation immediately by wire. Thank you.

Sincerely yours,

Sympathy

Dear Jill:

    Roy and I were deeply saddened by the news of Steve's sudden death. We valued his friendship for many years and will miss him very much.

    Our heartfelt sympathy goes out to you and your family. If we can help in any way at all in the weeks ahead, Jill, do let us know.

                          Sincerely,

Thank You

Dear Carl:

    I want to thank you for your hospitality during my recent visit to Atlanta. The time you spent introducing me to your associates and ushering me around your plant was highly informative and always enjoyable. You may be certain I greatly appreciated all your time and effort.

    Thanks ever so much, Carl. I'll be looking forward to seeing you in New York next month.

                          Best regards,

Chapter 10
Keeping Essential Records

To be well informed, a secretary needs to know something about the maintenance of certain books and records. Duties vary widely in this area, however. For some secretaries it is sufficient to have an intelligent understanding of basic financial matters and associated record-keeping procedures. For other secretaries it is important to be able to collect, record, and maintain essential books and records for an employer. Keeping track of financial transactions, tax data, and insurance records is a task requiring great care and accuracy. Errors in any of these areas can be costly, and a capable secretary learns how to avoid such problems.

HOW TO KEEP TAX RECORDS

Everyone is concerned with taxes—on a personal level if not on an organizational level. Thus a secretary, regardless of her current duties in the office, should keep abreast of changes in tax laws and know how to collect essential data. But some secretaries must do a lot more than this. They must record deductions, compute payments, process statements of receipts and expenditures, and even help make out tax returns. The tax records a secretary should know about basically consist of records and proof of expenditures and receipts, as explained below.

Recording Expenditures. Personal expenses to be recorded for income tax purposes are those expenses that are deductible on income tax returns. These include expenses for business trips; medical expenses; contributions; casualty and theft losses; interest expense; investment expenses; capital losses on property; bad debts; educational expenses; miscellaneous taxes such as those on real estate, gasoline, and personal property; professional costs such as office rent; and certain support payments such as alimony. Since tax laws change from year to year, a secretary should write each year to both the nearest Internal Revenue Service office and the state tax office for current information on deductible items.

You may be able to get the information to be recorded from forms given to you by your employer and others. Or you may simply have to go through the checkbook stubs periodically to find deductible items. In other cases, your employer may merely hand you a stack of receipts for bills that have been paid. The procedure will probably vary from item to item, and you will need to check all sources to be certain that you do not overlook any payment made by check or cash. After locating each payment, the deduction may be recorded on forms you prepare especially for each item (e.g., contributions) or on standard, loose-leaf accounting sheets with numerous columns that you keep in a three-ring binder. In addition to recording a description of an item and the amount spent for it, you must keep *proof* of each expenditure, for example, an invoice marked *PAID*. Many secretaries keep a folder of such items of proof for each category of deduction. Thus you might have a folder of receipted bills and other statements of proof for medical and drug expenses, one for business-trip expenses, another for professional costs such as rent, and so on. Each year new folders would be opened and the old ones retained in a permanent file for as long as current tax laws require proof of expenses and payments to be available.

Travel payments are frequently recorded initially on expense forms provided by the company or on standard forms purchased in office supply stores. But keep in mind that expenses reimbursed by the company are *not* deductible—only those for which your employer is not reimbursed are, and each of those expenses must be backed up by a proper receipt. Keeping track of profit and loss from investments and monitoring insurance payments are often primary record-keeping tasks by themselves (see How to Keep General Financial Records and How to Keep Insurance Records, below). Something such as a contribution, on the other hand, is usually handled more easily by keeping either a general listing of all contributions, totaled at year's end, or by recording individual listings per organization. For instance, all contributions during the year to the Cancer Society might go in a separate column especially marked *Cancer Society Donations.* A loose-leaf notebook with multicolumn sheets would probably serve best in these cases. **Many** other payments such as medical costs or professional expenses (rent, wages to employees, Social Security taxes paid on wages, expenses for professional journals, and so on) might also be recorded more easily on multicolumn forms or sheets. Experience will be your best guide in making up forms to record the payments or in setting up sheets with multiple columns for recording the deductible payments. In the meantime follow the underlying principle that each deductible item must be recorded and backed up by some type of proof of payment such as a bill marked *PAID*. It would be wise to type a list of probable deductions and ask your employer to add to or deduct from the list before setting up records and file folders.

Recording Income. Records of taxable income must be kept throughout the year the same as records of expenses. Income consists of wages, salaries, commissions, fees, royalties, and any other gross amounts received *before* deductions. It also includes cash dividends, interest received, capital gains on property, rental income, refunds and reimbursements, trust or estate funds, and pensions or annuities. Anything that must be reported as income on an income tax return should be recorded during the year. At the same time that you write each year to the nearest Internal Revenue Service office and the state tax office for current information on deductions, you should also request current information on taxable income.

As with expenditures, the information you need to record taxable income will come from different sources. Figures for compensation may come from W-2 forms, from miscellaneous checks received at irregular intervals, or from checks received at specific times during the year. Also as with expenditures, you will need to check all possible sources to be certain none is overlooked. Of course, in all such matters your employer will instruct you—or you should ask for a list of sources if none is given to you. Usually there will be a remittance statement or some form accompanying any check received. You may want to follow the same procedure used for expenses and set up a folder for each source of taxable income, filing all supporting documents in the appropriate folder. These, too, should be retained along with the expense folders for as long as current tax laws require documents to back up the information reported on income tax returns.

Income may be recorded on forms you design especially for each item (e.g., dividends received) or on standard multicolumn accounting sheets that you keep in a three-ring binder. (For a discussion of securities transactions, see How to Keep General Financial Records, page 243.) Wages and salaries are reported by a company at the end of a year, so no record of this income needs to be kept during the year. You will discover that many items involve both income and expenses. For instance, records of rentals for tax purposes must show not only the receipts but the related expenses such as building maintenance and real estate taxes. Even something such as royalties may include both income and expenses. The sale or exchange of property, too, involves a consideration of income and expense items, and complete and accurate records of both are needed to report a sale correctly when filing income tax returns. Whether the records you keep are relatively simple or very extensive depends on the complexity of your employer's personal and business transactions. But the objective is the same in either case: to record all taxable income and all allowable deductions and to file supporting documents and other evidence to back up each figure you record.

HOW TO KEEP GENERAL FINANCIAL RECORDS

At some point in their careers, many secretaries find they have become involved in their employer's financial activities. This may mean handling minor business transactions for the organization or keeping their employer's personal financial records. Because errors in this area can be so serious and costly, a capable secretary develops the habit of working carefully and double-checking everything she records. Something as simple as a misplaced decimal can make quite a difference ($10.00 *vs.* $100.0 *or* $1000.). You can see therefore how the careful working habits developed in keeping financial records are also valuable in all other phases of secretarial work. In addition to keeping tax records, described earlier, a secretary may be required to keep track of (1) securities transactions, (2) bank account transactions, and even (3) family financial matters.

Securities Transactions. Business and professional people frequently invest in stocks, bonds, mutual funds, and commodities. The secretary who assists in keeping track of securities transactions—particularly as they pertain to income taxes—will likely maintain several pertinent files, as well as record the actual purchase and sale transactions on a record form, card, or loose-leaf sheet. You might, for example, keep *investment literature* (prospectuses, reports, and so on) in one folder. Another folder might contain *statements* received from brokers. You might need two files for the transactions—one for *pending transactions* and another for *completed transactions. Corporate news* about the companies in which your employer has invested could go in a fifth folder. Finally, if activity warrants it, you may want a separate folder for filing notices and information concerning *expected income* from stocks and bonds. Each year new folders should be opened. Old files with financial information should be retained, but the folder with printed literature should be cleared out and updated periodically (ask your employer if he or she wants to retain any of the outdated literature).

In addition to keeping a record of purchases and sales, you should keep a regularly updated list of investments owned. Depending on the number of investments you are dealing with, this might be a single list of all investments (arranged alphabetically) or one list for stocks, another for bonds, and so forth. Either way, leave space between each letter of the alphabet to add new purchases during the year. A list of currently owned investments would include the following: name of security, number of shares, date purchased, cost per share, and total cost. If you set up this listing on multicolumn sheets, you can continue right across the page with data in additional columns pertaining to sales: date sold, gross sales price, commission, net proceeds, short-term gain/loss, and long-term gain/loss. Each year you should file the old list and start a new one, following the same procedure.

Some secretaries keep their record of transactions on cards filed in a small file box; others prefer standard, multicolumn, loose-leaf sheets retained in a three-ring binder. As another alternative, office supply stores have preprinted standard forms that are designed specifically to record security transactions. These records may vary in the amount of detail and type of information recorded, so you should consult your employer to determine exactly what he or she wants before purchasing a form or devising your own record. Most of the record forms, however, have space to describe the security at the top of the page or card: exchange listed on (e.g., New

York Stock Exchange), where kept, income tax status, date of issue, date of maturity, interest or dividend, when payable, and so forth. Beneath this are columns to show the details of each purchase and sale: security name, certificate number, number of shares, date purchased, from whom, date sold, to whom, cost per share, total cost, sales price, earnings, gain/loss, and so on. Regardless of the specific record form you purchase or make up, be certain to record full details on each transaction as soon as it occurs and you receive the information so that your employer's securities record will always be current.

Bank Account Transactions. Almost everyone is used to maintaining a checking account and a savings account. Thus secretarial procedures involving bank account transactions often seem more familiar than those concerning some of the other financial matters. Writing checks for your employer's signature, making deposits, and reconciling the bank statement are three routine secretarial duties. In some offices the secretary performs these tasks for different accounts. There may be a regular account for the larger transactions such as paying the rent and a special account for smaller transactions such as purchasing miscellaneous office supplies. If there is a savings account, the secretary may be expected to make deposits to it, too, and to verify statements (or passbook figures) of deposits, withdrawals, and interest accumulation. Most transactions, however, take place in the checking account(s).

When you write checks for someone else to sign, (1) fill out the check stub with enough information for a bookkeeper or accountant to use in recording entries of each payment in the books of account; (2) enter all deposits on the stub and see that the current balance is always carried forward; and (3) label each completed checkbook before filing it with the name of the bank, the account, and the dates of the first and last checks. The checks you draw for a signature must be completely legible. Type them if your handwriting is not perfectly clear. Double-check the date on the stub, comparing it against the information on the check. Use the full name of the payee but not a title such as *Mr.* or *Dr.* The amount on the right side of the check should be written with a decimal ($100.00) and on the full line beginning at the left with a diagonal (One Hundred and no/ 100-----Dollars). Use a dashed or broken line or dots to connect the cents to the word *Dollars*. Start as close to the left margin as possible each time so that no one can alter a check by writing in additional figures. For example, do not leave space for someone to change *$ 100.00* to *$2100.00* or to change *One Hundred* to *Two Thousand One Hundred*. Finally, before mailing the check, look to be certain that the signature is the same as that filed on the signature cards at the bank. When you spoil a check, you must write the word *Void* across its face, file it with the canceled checks, and cancel the stub as well, adjusting the balance on the next stub. To stop payment on a check, you must call the bank immediately, giving the name of the payee, the amount, and full information about the account (name, number, and so on). Follow up in writing.

Deposit slips as well as checks should be filled out clearly and accurately, using the printed slips supplied with the checks. Your office probably has a rubber stamp to use in endorsing checks. Endorsements are written or stamped on the back of the check across the left end. A typical *restrictive endorsement* is:

Pay to the order of
First National Bank of Baltimore
THE ABC COMPANY

With a *blank endorsement* you sign only your name on the back of the check. Should you lose it, however, anyone else can cash it by simply signing his or her name below yours. With a *specific endorsement* you sign the check over to someone else (Pay to the order of John Doe) and sign your name beneath those instructions.

Bank statements have a form, often on the reverse side, where you may reconcile your checkbook account with the current bank statement. To fill out this form, you need to compare the amount on each canceled check with the amount on your checkbook stub and on the statement. Each time the figures agree, you put a check mark beside them. After listing and deducting all outstanding checks and deposits and subtracting any debit memos or service charges, your checkbook balance should agree with the bank balance. Any error must be double-checked and then reported immediately to the bank. Also report any debit memo or service charge that seems unusual. As soon as the reconciliation is completed satisfactorily, you should initial it, date it, and file it (or give it to your employer if that is the practice in your office).

Family Financial Matters. The secretary who maintains financial records for her employer may also be asked to keep records of her employer's family expenses. This is often the case when the secretary records expense items that qualify as deductions on income tax returns. However, some employers want records of family financial matters for other reasons, too. Sometimes a person simply wants to know what things cost and where the money is going. Since each employer may have different reasons for recording family expenses, it is important to find out how much information is needed, in what areas, and for what purposes. Tax-deductible expenses, for instance, should be kept separate from other costs. Also, expenses to be reported on income tax returns must be kept separate for each family member in case each person files a separate return. (See How to Keep Tax Records, page 237, for further details on taxable income and deductible expenses.)

In addition to expenses recorded for tax purposes (wages, medical expenses, professional costs, contributions, and so on), your employer may want records of insurance (see How to Keep Insurance Records, page 252), clothing costs, recreation expenses, house maintenance and improvement costs and cost of household furnishings, travel expenses (for pleasure), automobile upkeep (personal), subscriptions and dues (nonbusiness), cost of hobbies, gift expenses, nondeductible taxes, cost of children's education, and so on. Be certain to distinguish between expenses that are legitimate business deductions (using the car to conduct business for the company) and nondeductible costs (driving the family to Yellowstone National Park).

Multiple-column loose-leaf sheets kept in a binder may be used for recording costs. One popular recording procedure is to set up one or several pages for each category of expense (for each person), such as clothing. For every expenditure, then, you would record the date of the check, charge payment, or cash expense; the check or charge account number, if any; a description of the payment (e.g., Howes Dept. Store—Donna's snowsuit); and the cost of the item. You might also have a *Totals* column, where you can add the total cost of clothing purchased at the end of each month. Some secretaries put tax-deductible items on the same sheet as the nondeductible items in the general record, but they also maintain a separate record of tax-deductible items only. This way an employer can see the overall cost picture from the general records and also check what is tax-deductible in the tax records. But ask your employer what he or she prefers and devise your own system accordingly.

HOW TO KEEP INSURANCE RECORDS

In some offices the secretary takes care of her employer's insurance records. This function may include making periodic premium payments on time to be certain all policies remain in force. It also may include having policies canceled or seeing that claims are filed. The secretary who sets up and maintains insurance records should make it a point to learn something about the principal types of insurance coverage such as life, basic and major medical, disability, and property insurance. In addition to setting up folders for the policies and related correspondence, a secretary needs to set up a good reminder system to insure that premiums are paid on time and to check on renewals of expiring contracts. Even though insurance companies send bills when payments are due, the alert secretary takes no chances. Although the types of reminder systems in use vary from office to office, many secretaries prefer a tickler card file (described in chapter 5) for insurance reminders, in conjunction with the usual reminder notations that are made on each person's calendar.

Life and Health Insurance Records. A *tickler card reminder system* consists of a card file with guides for each month and for each day of the month. A card, then, is placed behind the day a secretary wants to be reminded to do something, and each day she checks behind the current day's guide. If desired, she can simply move a card ahead behind another guide if it is necessary to check something again later. This type of system works well for certain types of life and health insurance. On each card to be used, the secretary types the policy name and number, name of the issuer, name of the insured, name of the agent, to whom the premium is payable, where to mail checks (or if payments are to be made automatically by the employer's bank), amount of the premium and whether dividends cover any portion of it, and due date of the premium.

The other essential record for life and health insurance is the *policy-description record.* There are a number of options available in setting up this record. You might use the same type of standard multiple-column sheet kept in a three-ring binder that you use for tax and other financial records. Or you might use a standard card or sheet record sold by office suppliers. Or you might devise your own form. Policy records typically show facts such as the insurance company's name, agent's name, policy number, type of policy (e.g., major medical), date of issue, age at issue, expiration date, gross amount of insurance coverage or income payments, premium amount, premium due date, beneficiary, and cash surrender value. If your employer wants a more detailed record, you can simply add more columns to show things such as the amount of dividends and the rate of dividends. You can also set up a distribution record, with a column for each day of the month where you record the amount of the premium paid for each policy on a monthly basis. Ask your employer what information he or she needs for policy-description and payment-distribution records.

Property Insurance Records. Businesses and individuals both need property insurance—for buildings, materials and supplies, fixtures, automobiles, and so on.

Although agents and insurance companies send notices of renewals before expiration dates, the secretary who keeps property insurance records does not rely solely on such notices. Reminder systems are needed for property insurance just as they are for life and health insurance. Again, a tickler card file is a convenient system for keeping track of expiration dates of the various types of insurance policies. Each card needs to show the insurer's name, agent's name, insured person's name, policy number, type of policy (e.g., automobile) and property covered, amount of premium, and expiration date. Check the file daily, and if a renewal for any policy is not received on time, contact your employer's agent right away.

You should keep a record of each type of property insurance just as you keep a policy-description record for each life and health policy. A property insurance record can be set up on multicolumn looseleaf sheets and kept in a binder or on a specially prepared card or form. Also, office suppliers often sell standard forms designed for policies other than life insurance contracts. The form you use will probably have a column for the name of the insurance company, agent's name, policy number, kind of insurance, beginning and expiration dates, type of property covered and where located, gross amount of coverage, premium, and date premium is paid. Some forms provide much more detail, with space to record dividends, rate of dividend, net premium, cancellation date, type and cost of improvements, and so on. Check with your employer to determine the type of record you should keep and whether a separate record form is needed for detailed information on each property or whether descriptions can be listed together for all property on one form. Your employer may also want a separate form with columns for each month to show the distribution of payments for general insurance. This type of payment-distribution record would be similar to the one to record payments for life insurance premiums, described above. Since duties vary so much in the record-keeping area, secretaries should work closely with their employers in devising forms and establishing record-keeping procedures.

Chapter 11

Finding Useful Information Sources

In a busy office the less time it takes to locate information, the better. The only way to find facts and figures quickly is to know where to go, and this includes organizations as well as publications. Secretaries have many occasions to undertake both limited fact finding and extensive research. A client may pose a question that prompts you to investigate something. Your employer may ask you to help collect information for a report. You may be preparing a recommendation, background paper, or report of your own. Although there are many direct needs, you also may be looking for sources of information simply to become better informed. No matter what the motive is, there is no question that you will be more of an asset to your employer if you know where to find useful information.

ORGANIZATIONS

Most people who need to locate information think of going to the library. Although library research is often necessary and appropriate, it may not be the only alternative. Some secretaries forget that their own organizations are often excellent sources of information. Even in a small firm, other persons and departments must collect data, too. When employees have good working relations, they are usually happy to be of help and exchange information. Manufacturers and distributors of products and literature are also logical sources for certain types of information. The telephone directory Yellow Pages will give you names, addresses, and phone numbers of local manufacturers, suppliers, newspapers, and so on.

Some of the best sources of information are the specialized organizations scattered across the nation, frequently with chapters or branches in major metropolitan areas. These are the (1) governmental agencies; (2) trade associations and professional societies; (3) colleges, universities, and trade schools; (4) research institutes; and (5) local clubs and civic groups. It may be frustrating at times to locate the right person to speak with, but, then, effective research often demands persistence. Some organizations have a public information office. Otherwise, if you do not know the best person or department to contact, try the public relations office. The personnel there are responsible for generating news about their organization and may have what you need or be able to refer you to someone else. Keep in mind that you may be able to receive free advice and literature up to a point, but most organizations do not have the time or staff to do extensive research for everyone who calls. If you are uncertain, ask in advance whether there will be a charge for any information you receive.

Government Agencies. The *government* has always been a good source of information. Many departments and agencies publish reports and bulletins that are on sale through the Superintendent of Documents at the U.S. Government Printing Office in Washington, D.C. (See also Governmental Data, page 274.) Often the title of the agency is a good clue about the subject matter you might pursue, for example: Agricultural Research Service, Commission on Civil Rights, Federal Aviation Agency, International Atomic Energy Agency, National Institutes of

Health, and Public Housing Administration. The *U.S. Government Organization Manual* (see Directories and Indexes, below) has a list of all federal agencies. You may also be able to find listings in your local library. If you frequently use government agencies as a source of information, you may want to secure a current Washington, D.C., telephone directory through your local telephone company business office.

Trade and Professional Associations. For almost every product or service, there is a *trade or professional association* organized to serve the needs of interested members. Membership is not always limited to those who manufacture and/or sell the product or service. Sometimes the association will admit anyone who is merely interested in the product or service for whatever reason. Publications are often offered for sale to anyone who wants to buy them. Most trade and professional associations publish something: bulletins, newsletters, magazines or journals, conference proceedings, books, and so on. The literature published by an association can be valuable to a researcher. But sometimes even more important are the members themselves. In other words, each member is an excellent source of information in addition to the association's administration. By contacting the association headquarters (or a local chapter office), you may find what you want to know or be referred to a member organization that has the information you need. Like the names of government agencies, the names of associations indicate the area of interest, for example: American Automobile Association, American Medical Association, American Society of Civil Engineers, American Society of Travel Agents, and National Education Association. Local associations or chapters of national associations will be listed in the telephone directory Yellow Pages. Consult a directory of associations (see Directories and Indexes, below) for a complete list of all trade associations and professional societies.

Colleges, Universities, and Trade Schools. What better source of information could you find for a particular subject than the person who teaches it? Wherever you live, there is probably at least one *college* or *trade school* nearby and a number of larger *universities* located throughout your state. Where to go depends, of course, on the subject you are investigating. If you want to know something about electrical wiring, a trade or vocational school specializing in this general area might be the best source. Telephone and other directories will indicate what specialties such schools provide. Sometimes the name of the school will tell you, for example, Thomas Secretarial Studio. Subject areas such as history or biology are covered by colleges and universities. There may be a complete department devoted to the general subject area (Department of Geography) or at least one or two persons who teach the specific subject that interests you (professor of geomorphology). Most trade school instructors and college professors not only have an in-depth knowledge of their area of expertise but also know where to go to find out more. Another advantage to this source of information is the school library. If your local public library is inadequate for your needs, you may be able to use the library facilities of a nearby school or university. The nice thing about colleges, universities, and trade schools is that there are so many avenues to explore within the one institution. (See Directories and Indexes, below, for guides that list public and private educational institutions.)

Research Institutes. The word *institute* is used by associations, colleges, governmental agencies, and private facilities. Therefore the use of this word in an organization's title may not be an indication that it is devoted primarily to research. But many of the organizations known as institutes do conduct research on a large scale. Some names are familiar, for example, the Salk Institute. But if you scan the listings in your local Yellow Pages or in various governmental and educational directories, you may find many others less familiar but nevertheless good sources of information. Some of these organizations work in areas of advanced technologies—nuclear energy, mind control, and so on. When their efforts are ready for public release, they may be published as reports, as articles in scientific journals, as papers presented at conferences, or as books. Because the organizations are devoted to research, they have extensive files, studies, and other data at their disposal. How much is available free or for sale to the public depends strictly on the subject, the level of development, and the particular institute. In any case this is clearly a good source area for various types of information, and it is well worth pursuing.

Local Clubs and Civic Groups. No one thinks much about clubs and civic groups for fact-finding activities. But these organizations are surprisingly good sources of information for certain subject matter. Moreover, since they are local organizations, you may be able to attend meetings as a guest, interview members, and borrow literature for further study. Examples of *civic organizations* are the League of Women Voters, City Ballet Company, City Collection (or Credit) Bureau, General Assembly of Churches, and City Civic Foundation. Usually there are even more *local clubs* of all types, such as the City AAA Automobile Association, Athletic Club, City Country Club, Gun Club, and Kiwanis Club. All of the civic groups and clubs located in your city will be listed in your telephone directory Yellow Pages.

PUBLICATIONS

Any search for information will likely lead to printed materials: reports, bulletins, newsletters, magazines, journals, booklets, manuals, books, and any other type of published or unpublished literature. The publications you consult may be found in a variety of places. Many will be in public, school, company, state, or research organization libraries. Others may be on sale or offered free through the mail. Some will be available only by subscription or club membership. Certain reference sources are so large, possibly containing numerous volumes, and thus so expensive that you would not want to purchase them. Although your employer may want to add various books and periodicals to the office library, many of the publications you consult on fact-finding missions will probably be in someone else's library. To help you find information easily and quickly, you should visit nearby libraries and become familiar with their reference rooms, the vertical files (for pamphlets and so on), and the card catalogs (for books). Whether you purchase a book or consult it in a library, always use the latest edition.

The following sections describe some of the major sources of information: (1) dictionaries, (2) encyclopedias, (3) almanacs and yearbooks, (4) atlases, (5) directories and indexes, (6) newspapers and periodicals, (7) biographical references, (8) style and word-usage books, (9) books of quotations, (10) industry and financial information, and (11) governmental data. In addition to general reference sources, libraries also have sources of information related to a particular industry or profession. For instance, the dictionaries listed below are only a few of the many general abridged and unabridged editions published. But you can also find specialized dictionaries, for example, *Black's Law Dictionary,* West Publishing Company, St. Paul, Minnesota.

Dictionaries

The American Heritage Dictionary of the English Language, American Heritage Publishing Co., New York.

50,000 Words Divided and Spelled, Follett Publishing Company, Chicago.

Follett Vest-Pocket Webster Dictionary, Follett Publishing Company, Chicago.

Funk & Wagnall's Standard College Dictionary, Funk & Wagnalls Co., New York.

The Random House Dictionary of the English Language (unabridged), Random House, New York.

Webster's New Collegiate Dictionary, G. & C. Merriam Co., Springfield, Mass.

Webster's New International Dictionary (unabridged), G. & C. Merriam Co., Springfield, Mass.

Encyclopedias

Collier's Encyclopedia, The Crowell-Collier Publishing Co., New York.

Columbia Encyclopedia, 1 vol., Columbia University Press, New York.

Encyclopaedia Britannica, Encyclopaedia Britannica, Inc., Chicago.

Encyclopedia Americana, Americana Corp., New York.

Grolier Encyclopedia, The Grolier Society, New York.

Almanacs and Yearbooks

Information Please Almanac, Simon and Schuster, New York (annually).

Reader's Digest Almanac and Yearbook, Funk & Wagnalls Co., New York (annually).

Statistical Abstract of the United States, U.S. Government Printing Office, Washington, D.C. (annually).

Statistical Yearbook, United Nations, New York (annually).

The World Almanac and Book of Facts, Doubleday & Co., Garden City, N.Y. (annually).

Atlases

Encyclopaedia Britannica World Atlas, Encyclopaedia Britannica, Inc., Chicago.

Hammond Contemporary World Atlas, Doubleday & Co., Garden City, N.Y.

Rand McNally Commercial Atlas and Marketing Guide, Rand McNally & Co., Chicago (annually).

Rand McNally Road Atlas, Rand McNally & Co., Chicago (annually).

Directories and Indexes

American Medical Directory, American Medical Association, Chicago (annually; lists physicians in the U.S. and Canada plus data on schools and publications).

Applied Science and Technology Index, H. W. Wilson Co., New York (throughout the year; lists periodicals in technical and scientific fields).

Books in Print, R. R. Bowker Co., New York (annually; author-title-subject index to books).

Business Periodicals Index, H. W. Wilson Co., New York (throughout the year; lists periodicals in business subject areas).

Directory of Corporations, Directors and Executives, Standard and Poor's Corp., McGraw-Hill, New York (3 vol. set, with annual supplements).

Gale's Encyclopedia of Associations, Gale Research Co., Detroit (guide to national associations, societies, federations, and other nonprofit organizations).

Hotel and Motel Red Book, American Hotel Association Directory Corp., New York (annually; alphabetical list of members of the American Hotel and Motel Association).

Martindale-Hubbell Law Directory, Martindale-Hubbell, Inc., Summit, N.J. (annually; lists lawyers and digests of laws).

N. W. Ayer & Son's Directory of Newspapers and Periodicals, N. W. Ayer & Son, Philadelphia (lists publications and describes areas where they are marketed).

New York Times Index, The New York Times Co., New York (monthly).

Official Airline Guide, R. H. Donnelley, Chicago (bimonthly; lists U.S. and foreign schedules and fares).

Official Congressional Directory, U.S. Government Printing Office, Washington, D.C. (lists governmental officials and members of the press).

Official Guide of the Railways, National Railway Publications Co., New York (lists schedules and timetables of all railroads in the U.S., Canada, and Mexico).

Patterson's American Education, Educational Directories, Mount Prospect, Ill. (annually; lists and describes public, private, and special schools and educational associations).

Periodicals: Price List 36, U.S. Government Printing Office, Washington, D.C. (lists all periodicals published by the U.S. government).

Reader's Guide to Periodical Literature, H. W. Wilson Co., New York (throughout the year; index to general, nontechnical periodicals in the U.S.).

Thomas' Register of American Manufacturers, Thomas Publishing Co., New York (annually).

Ulrich's International Periodicals Directory, R. R. Bowker Co., New York (lists scientific, medical, and technical periodicals in one volume and arts, humanities, business, and social sciences in another volume).

U.S. Government Organization Manual, U.S. Government Printing Office, Washington, D.C. (lists and describes federal agencies).

Wall Street Journal Index, Dow Jones and Co., New York (monthly, with annual cumulations).

Newspapers and Periodicals

Business Week, McGraw-Hill, New York (weekly).

Dun's Review, Dun & Bradstreet, New York (monthly).

Fortune, Time, Inc., New York (monthly).

Nation's Business, Chamber of Commerce of the United States, Washington, D.C. (monthly).

New York Times, The New York Times Co., New York (daily).

Survey of Current Business, U.S. Department of Commerce, Washington, D.C. (weekly).

Wall Street Journal, Dow Jones and Co., New York (daily).

Biographical References

Current Biography, H. W. Wilson Co., New York (monthly; cumulated in yearbooks, which have editions for different fields).

Dictionary of American Biography, Charles Scribner's Sons, New York (multivolume set).

Webster's Biographical Dictionary, G. & C. Merriam Co., Springfield, Mass.

Who's Who, A. N. Marquis Co., Chicago (volumes on who's who in America, of American women, in commerce and industry, and in the East, West, and so on).

Style and Word-Usage Books

The Elements of Style, Macmillan, New York.

A Dictionary of Contemporary American Usage, Random House, New York.

A Dictionary of Modern English Usage, H. W. Fowler, London.

Funk & Wagnalls Modern Guide to Synonyms, Funk & Wagnalls Co., New York.

A Manual of Style, University of Chicago Press, Chicago.

New York Times Style Book for Writers and Editors, McGraw-Hill, New York.

Roget's International Thesaurus, Thomas Y. Crowell Co., New York.

Webster's New Dictionary of Synonyms, G. & C. Merriam Co., Springfield, Mass.

Word Finder, Prentice-Hall, Englewood Cliffs, N.J.

Words into Type, Appleton-Century-Crofts, New York.

Books of Quotations

Bartlett's Familiar Quotations, Little, Brown and Co., Boston.

March's Thesaurus and Dictionary of the English Language, Doubleday & Co., Garden City, N.Y.

The New Book of Unusual Quotations,

Harper & Row, Publishers, New York.

The Oxford Dictionary of Quotations, Oxford University Press, New York.

Industry and Financial Information

The Conference Board Business Record, National Industrial Conference Board, New York (monthly).

Consumer Reports, Consumers Union of U.S., Mount Vernon, N.Y. (monthly reports on products).

Current Industrial Reports, U.S. Department of Commerce, Washington, D.C. (quarterly or throughout the year; covering various industries such as metalworking).

Dun & Bradstreet Reference Book, Dun & Bradstreet, New York (bimonthly credit ratings).

Economic Indicators, U.S. Government Printing Office, Washington, D.C. (monthly).

Federal Reserve Bulletin, Federal Reserve System, Washington, D.C. (monthly).

Moody's Investor Service, New York (manuals such as *Moody's Bond Record, Manual of Investments, Industrial Manual, Handbook of Common Stocks*).

Prentice-Hall Federal Tax Guide, Prentice-Hall, Englewood Cliffs, N.J. (annual, with supplements).

Standard and Poor's Corporation, New York (guides and services such as *Standard Corporation Records,* daily; *Standard and Poor's Trade and Securities Service,* weekly; and *Standard and Poor's Bond Guide,* monthly).

Value Line, Arnold Bernhard and Co., New York (loose-leaf service).

Governmental Data

Congressional Record, U.S. Government Printing Office, Washington, D.C. (annually; proceedings).

Directory of International Mail, U.S. Government Printing Office, Washington, D.C.

The Monthly Catalog of United States Government Publications, U.S. Government Printing Office, Washington, D.C. (with annual cumulations).

Postal Manual, U.S. Government Printing Office, Washington, D.C.

Selected United States Government Publications, U.S. Government Printing Office, Washington, D.C. (free semimonthly list).

Survey of Federal Publications, Small

Business Administration, Washington, D.C.

U.S. Government Printing Office Price Lists, U.S. Government Printing Office, Washington, D.C. (free lists of publications for sale in all areas—finance, education, occupations, patents, aviation, and so on).

UN Monthly Chronicle, United Nations, New York (monthly).

Guide to Miscellaneous Data

Two-Letter Postal Abbreviations

Alabama	AL
Alaska	AK
Arizona	AZ
Arkansas	AR
California	CA
Colorado	CO
Connecticut	CT
Delaware	DE
District of Columbia	DC
Florida	FL
Georgia	GA
Hawaii	HI
Idaho	ID
Illinois	IL
Indiana	IN
Iowa	IA
Kansas	KS
Kentucky	KY
Louisiana	LA
Maine	ME
Maryland	MD

Massachusetts	MA
Michigan	MI
Minnesota	MN
Mississippi	MS
Missouri	MO
Montana	MT
Nebraska	NE
Nevada	NV
New Hampshire	NH
New Jersey	NJ
New Mexico	NM
New York	NY
North Carolina	NC
North Dakota	ND
Ohio	OH
Oklahoma	OK
Oregon	OR
Pennsylvania	PA
Puerto Rico	PR
Rhode Island	RI
South Carolina	SC
South Dakota	SD
Tennessee	TN
Texas	TX
Utah	UT
Vermont	VT
Virgin Islands	VI
Virginia	VA
Washington	WA
West Virginia	WV
Wisconsin	WI
Wyoming	WY

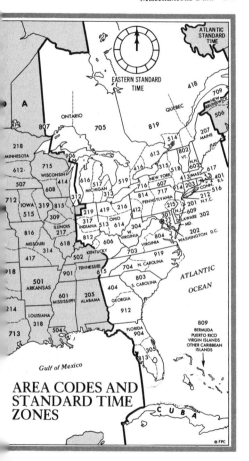

AREA CODES AND
STANDARD TIME
ZONES

Proofreader Marks

In Margin	In Text	Meaning
e	The minutess ✓	Delete
ℰ	The minuutes	Delete and close up
stet	yesterday's call	Let it stand
no #	for you.) ¶Afterwards we	No paragraph
#	Hisreport	Add space
out, sc	Small ∧	Something missing; see copy
sp out	10 eet	Spell out
⌢	secre tary	Close up
⊏	His house	Move left
⊐	His house	Move right
tr	Sany Mason	Transpose
‖	‖ Telephone and ‖ Electric Company	Line up
⧺	day. But it	New paragraph
⑦	1777 ∧	Question to author
?	Is it true ∧	Insert question mark
!	Wonderful ∧	Insert exclamation
=	self confident	Insert hyphen
∨ ∨	He said, Yes. ∧	Insert quotation marks
⌃ ⸵	hard yet it	Insert semicolon
⸲	the following ∧	Insert colon
⌃ ⊙	four, five and six	Insert comma
⊙	I do ∧	Insert period
∨	Janes ∧	Insert apostrophe

Proofreader Marks

In Margin	In Text	Meaning
f/	f̸ar	Change to f
caps (or ≡)	michael	Set in capital letters
lc	her P̸lan	Set in lowercase letters
bf (or ~~~)	West vs. East	Set in boldface type
ital. (or __)	Webster's Dictionary	Set in italic type
S.C. (or =)	Spain	Set in small capitals
c.+s.c.	spain	Set in caps and small caps
√√	We do n̸o̸t	Correct uneven spacing
6	d̸oy	Upside down
□	□They think	Indent one em
Rom	(morning)	Change to roman face
³ˇ	address. ˇ3ˇ	Set as superior number
₂^	H₂O	Set as inferior number
⊏/⊐	∧x + y∧	Insert brackets
(/)	∧a + b∧	Insert parentheses
—M	signs—now	One-em dash

Correct Forms of Address

The forms of address shown here are general guides to correct usage for persons holding a professional, honorary, or official title. (See Using the Correct Forms of Address, chapter 9, for general rules concerning the use of *Mr., Mrs., Miss,* and *Ms.* in business correspondence.) Although many of the positions referred to below are held by both men and women, most of the examples show the correct forms of address for men. When a woman holds the same position, you would substitute *Madam* for *Sir* and *Mrs., Miss,* or *Ms.* for *Mr.* When someone holds a military title, use it in place of *The Honorable.* Also, governors of some states (Massachusetts by law and other states by courtesy) are addressed as *His (or Her) Excellency* instead of *The Honorable.* Some British titles differ from the traditional usage, too. For instance, a representative from Great Britain is the *British Ambassador* or *British Minister* in place of *Ambassador (Minister) of (Country)* as used elsewhere. Royalty, of course, requires the use of *His (or Her) Excellency* in diplomatic titles instead of *The Honorable.* Another exception to a general rule is that in Latin American countries the title *Ambassador (Minister) of the United States of America* is preferred rather than *American Ambassador (Minister),* which is customary in most other cases.

The forms of address illustrated below include those for the following: The

White House (see below); The Federal Judiciary (page 285); Members of Congress (page 287); Heads of Congressional Agencies (page 291); Executive Department Officials (page 292); Other Agency Heads (page 293); Ambassadors and Ministers (page 295); United Nations Officials (page 297); State and Local Officials (page 299); The Clergy (page 302); Army, Air Force, and Marine Corps (page 309); Navy and Coast Guard (page 311); Service Academy Members (page 312); and Academic Titles (page 312).

The White House

The President:	The President The White House Washington, D.C. 20025
	Mr. President: (formal) Dear Mr. President: (informal)
	Respectfully yours, (formal) Sincerely yours, (informal)
Wife of the President:	Mrs. (full married name) The White House Washington, D.C. 20025
	Dear Mrs. (surname):
	Sincerely yours,

Assistant to the President:	The Honorable (full name) Assistant to the President The White House Washington, D.C. 20025 Dear Mr. (surname): Sincerely yours,
Secretary to the President:	The Honorable (full name) Secretary to the President The White House Washington, D.C. 20025 Dear Mr. (surname): Sincerely yours,
The Vice-President:	The Vice-President of the United States United States Senate Washington, D.C. 20025 Mr. Vice-President: (formal) Dear Mr. Vice-President: (informal) Very truly yours, (formal) Sincerely yours, (informal)

The Federal Judiciary

The Chief Justice of the Supreme Court:	The Chief Justice of the United States The Supreme Court of the United States Washington, D.C. 20025
	Sir: (formal) Dear Mr. Chief Justice: (informal)
	Very truly yours, (formal) Sincerely yours, (informal)
Associate Justice of the Supreme Court:	Mr. Justice (surname) The Supreme Court of the United States Washington, D.C. 20025
	Sir: (formal) Dear Mr. Justice: (informal)
	Very truly yours, (formal) Sincerely yours, (informal)
Retired Justice of the Supreme Court:	The Honorable (full name) (Local address)
	Sir: (formal) Dear Mr. Justice: (informal)

	Very truly yours, (formal) Sincerely yours, (informal)
Presiding Justice of Other Federal Courts:	The Honorable (full name) Presiding Justice (Name of court) (Local address)
	Sir: (formal) Dear Mr. Justice: (informal)
	Very truly yours, (formal) Sincerely yours, (informal)
Judge of a Federal Court:	The Honorable (full name) Judge of the (name of court; if a U.S. district court, give district) (Local address)
	Dear Judge (surname):
	Sincerely yours,
Clerk of a Federal Court:	(Full name), Esquire Clerk of the (name of court; if a U.S. district court, give district) (Local address)
	Dear Mr. (surname):
	Sincerely yours,

Members of Congress

Committee Chairman, United States Senate:

The Honorable (full name)
Chairman, Committee on (name)
United States Senate
Washington, D.C. 20025

Dear Mr. Chairman:

Sincerely yours,

Chairman of a Joint Committee:

The Honorable (full name)
Chairman, Joint Committee on (name)
Congress of the United States
Washington, D.C. 20025

Dear Mr. Chairman:

Sincerely yours,

Subcommittee Chairman, United States Senate:

The Honorable (full name)
Chairman, Subcommittee on (name)
(Name of parent committee)
United States Senate
Washington, D.C. 20025

Dear Senator (surname):

Sincerely yours,

Senator (Washington, D.C., Office):	The Honorable (full name) United States Senate Washington, D.C. 20025
	Dear Senator (surname):
	Sincerely yours,
Senator (Away from Washington, D.C.):	The Honorable (full name) United States Senator (Local address)
	Dear Senator (surname):
	Sincerely yours,
Former Senator:	The Honorable (full name) (Local address)
	Dear Senator (surname):
	Sincerely yours,
Office of Deceased Senator:	Secretary to the late Senator (full name) United States Senate Washington, D.C. 20025
	Dear Mr. (surname):
	Sincerely yours,

| Speaker of the House of Representatives: | The Honorable (full name) Speaker of the House of Representatives Washington, D.C. 20025

Sir: (formal) Dear Mr. Speaker: (informal)

Very truly yours, (formal) Sincerely yours, (informal) |
|---|---|
| Committee Chairman, House of Representatives: | The Honorable (full name) Chairman, Committee on (name) House of Representatives Washington, D.C. 20025

Dear Mr. Chairman:

Sincerely yours, |
| Subcommittee Chairman, House of Representatives: | The Honorable (full name) Chairman, Subcommittee on (name) (Name of parent committee) House of Representatives |

Washington, D.C.
20025

Dear Mr. (surname):

Sincerely yours,

Representative
(Washington, D.C.,
Office):

The Honorable (full
name)
House of
Representatives
Washington, D.C.
20025

Dear Mr. (surname):

Sincerely yours,

Representative
(Away from
Washington, D.C.):

The Honorable (full
name)
Representative in
Congress
(Local address)

Dear Mr. (surname):

Sincerely yours,

Office of a Deceased
Representative:

Secretary to the late
(full name)
House of
Representatives
Washington, D.C.
20025

Dear Mr. (surname):

Sincerely yours,

Resident
Commissioner:

The Honorable (full
name)
Resident
Commissioner of
(name of area)

House of
  Representatives
Washington, D.C.
  20025

Dear Mr. (surname):

Sincerely yours,

Heads of Congressional Agencies

Librarian of Congress:	The Honorable (full name) Librarian of Congress Library of Congress Washington, D.C. 20025 Dear Mr. (surname): Sincerely yours,
Comptroller General (Head of the General Accounting Office):	The Honorable (full name) Comptroller General of the United States General Accounting Office Washington, D.C. 20025 Dear Mr. (surname): Sincerely yours,
Public Printer (Head of the U.S. Government Printing Office):	The Honorable (full name) Public Printer U.S. Government Printing Office

Washington, D.C. 20025

Dear Mr. (surname):

Sincerely yours,

Executive Department Officials

Members of the Cabinet of Rank of "Secretary":

The Honorable (full name)
Secretary of (name of department)
Washington, D.C. 20025

Dear Mr. Secretary:

Sincerely yours,

Postmaster General (Head of the U.S. Postal Service):

The Honorable (full name)
Postmaster General
Washington, D.C. 20025

Dear Mr. Postmaster General:

Sincerely yours,

Attorney General (Head of the Department of Justice):

The Honorable (full name)
The Attorney General
Washington, D.C. 20025

Dear Mr. Attorney General:

Sincerely yours,

Under Secretary of a Department:	The Honorable (full name)
	Under Secretary of (name of department)
	Washington, D.C. 20025
	Dear Mr. (surname):
	Sincerely yours,
Deputy Secretary of a Department:	The Honorable (full name)
	Deputy Secretary of (name of department)
	Washington, D.C. 20025
	Dear Mr. (surname):
	Sincerely yours,
Assistant Secretary of a Department:	The Honorable (full name)
	Assistant Secretary of (name of department)
	Washington, D.C. 20025
	Dear Mr. (surname):
	Sincerely yours,

Other Agency Heads

| Director of the Bureau of the Budget: | The Honorable (full name) |
| | Director |

Bureau of the
  Budget
Washington, D.C.
  20025

Dear Mr. (surname):

Sincerely yours,

Head of a Federal
Authority or Board:

The Honorable (full
  name)
(Title)
(Name of agency)
Washington, D.C.
  20025

Dear Mr. (surname):

Sincerely yours,

President of a
Commission:

The Honorable (full
  name)
President
(Name of
  commission)
Washington, D.C.
  20025

Dear Mr. (surname):

Sincerely yours,

Chairman of a
Commission:

The Honorable (full
  name)
Member
(Name of
  commission)
Washington, D.C.
  20025

Dear Mr. (surname):

Sincerely yours,

Chairman of a
Board:

The Honorable (full
name)
Chairman
(Name of board)
Washington, D.C.
20025

Dear Mr. Chairman:

Sincerely yours,

Ambassadors and Ministers

Ambassador:

The Honorable (full
name)
American
Ambassador
(City), (country)

Sir: (formal)
Dear Mr.
Ambassador:
(informal)

Very truly yours,
(formal)
Sincerely yours,
(informal)

Minister:

The Honorable (full
name)
American Minister
(City), (country)

Sir: (formal)
Dear Mr. Minister:
(informal)

Very truly yours,
(formal)
Sincerely yours,
(informal)

Chargé d'Affaires, Consul General, Consul, or Vice Consul:	(Full name), Esquire (Title) (City), (country)
	Sir: (formal) Dear Mr. (surname): (informal)
	Very truly yours, (formal) Sincerely yours, (informal)
Foreign Ambassador in the United States:	His Excellency, (full name) Ambassador of (country) (Local address)
	Excellency: (formal) Dear Mr. Ambassador: (informal)
	Very truly yours, (formal) Sincerely yours, (informal)
Foreign Minister in the United States:	The Honorable (full name) Minister of (country) (Local address)
	Sir: (formal) Dear Mr. Minister: (informal)
	Very truly yours, (formal) Sincerely yours, (informal)

Foreign Chargé d'Affaires in the United States:	Mr. (full name) Chargé d'Affaires of (country) (Local address)
	Sir: (formal) Dear Mr. (surname): (informal)
	Very truly yours, (formal) Sincerely yours, (informal)

United Nations Officials

Secretary General of the United Nations:	His Excellency, (full name) Secretary General of the United Nations New York, N.Y. 10016
	Excellency: (formal) Dear Mr. Secretary General: (informal)
	Very truly yours, (formal) Sincerely yours, (informal)
Under Secretary of the United Nations:	The Honorable (full name) Under Secretary in Charge of (name of office or body) United Nations New York, N.Y. 10016

Sir: (formal)
Dear Mr. (surname):
(informal)

Very truly yours,
(formal)
Sincerely yours,
(informal)

U.S. Representative
with Rank of
Ambassador:

The Honorable (full
name)
United States
Representative to
the United
Nations
New York, N.Y.
10016

Sir: (formal)
Dear Mr.
Ambassador:
(informal)

Very truly yours,
(formal)
Sincerely yours,
(informal)

Foreign
Representative with
Rank of
Ambassador:

His Excellency, (full
name)
Representative of
(country) to the
United Nations
New York, N.Y.
10016

Excellency: (formal)
Dear Mr.
Ambassador:
(informal)

Very truly yours,
(formal)

Sincerely yours,
(informal)

State and Local Officials

Governor of a State:

The Honorable (full name)
Governor of (state)
(City), (state)

Sir: (formal)
Dear Governor (surname): (informal)

Respectfully yours, (formal)
Very sincerely yours, (informal)

Acting Governor of a State:

The Honorable (full name)
Acting Governor of (state)
(City), (state)

Sir: (formal)
Dear Mr. (surname): (informal)

Respectfully yours, (formal)
Very sincerely yours, (informal)

Lieutenant Governor of a State:

The Honorable (full name)
Lieutenant Governor of (state)
(City), (state)

Dear Mr. (surname):

Sincerely yours,

Secretary of State of a State:	The Honorable (full name): Secretary of State of (state) (City), (state)
	Dear Mr. Secretary:
	Sincerely yours,
Chief Justice of the Supreme Court of a State:	The Honorable (full name) Chief Justice of the Supreme Court of (state) (City), (state)
	Sir: (formal) Dear Mr. Chief Justice: (informal)
	Very truly yours, (formal) Sincerely yours, (informal)
Attorney General of a State:	The Honorable (full name) Attorney General of (state) (City), (state)
	Dear Mr. Attorney General:
	Sincerely yours,
Treasurer, Comptroller, or Auditor of a State:	The Honorable (full name) (Title) of the State of (state) (City), (state)

Dear Mr. (surname):

Sincerely yours,

President of the Senate of a State:	The Honorable (full name) President of the Senate of the State of (state) (City), (state)

Dear Mr. (surname):

Sincerely yours,

State Senator:	The Honorable (full name) The State Senate (City), (state)

Dear Mr. (surname):

Sincerely yours,

Speaker of the House of Representatives or of the Assembly or of the House of Delegates of a State:	The Honorable (full name) Speaker of the House of Representatives (or Assembly or House of Delegates) of the State of (state) (City), (state)

Dear Mr. (surname):

Sincerely yours,

State Representative, Assemblyman, or Delegate:	The Honorable (full name) House of Representatives (or Assembly or House of Delegates) (City), (state)

Dear Mr. (surname):

Sincerely yours,

Mayor:

The Honorable (full name)
Mayor of (name of city)
(City), (state)

Dear Mayor (surname):

Sincerely yours,

President of a Board of Commissioners:

The Honorable (full name)
President
Board of Commissioners of (name of city)
(City), (state)

Dear Mr. (surname):

Sincerely yours,

The Clergy

Minister, Pastor, or Rector (with Doctoral Degree):

The Reverend (full name)
(Title), (name of church)
(Local address)

Dear Dr. (surname):

Sincerely yours,

Minister, Pastor, or Rector (without Doctoral Degree):

The Reverend (full name)
(Title), (name of church)
(Local address)

Dear Mr. (surname):

Sincerely yours,

Rabbi (with Doctoral Degree):	Rabbi (full name) (Local address)
	Dear Dr. (surname):
	Sincerely yours,
Rabbi (without Doctoral Degree):	Rabbi (full name) (Local address)
	Dear Rabbi (surname):
	Sincerely yours,
Catholic Cardinal:	His Eminence (Christian name) Cardinal (surname) Archbishop of (province) (or Bishop of, if a bishop or archbishop) (Local address)
	Your Eminence: (formal) Dear Cardinal (surname): (informal)
	Respectfully yours, (formal) Sincerely yours, (informal)
Catholic Archbishop:	The Most Reverend (full name)

Archbishop of
(province)
(Local address)

Your Excellency:
(formal)
Dear Archbishop
(surname):
(informal)

Respectfully yours,
(formal)
Sincerely yours,
(informal)

Catholic Bishop: The Most Reverend
(full name)
Bishop of (province)
(Local address)

Your Excellency:
(formal)
Dear Bishop
(surname):
(informal)

Respectfully yours,
(formal)
Sincerely yours,
(informal)

Catholic Abbot: The Right Reverend
(full name)
Abbot of (name of
abbey)
(Local address)

Dear Father Abbot:
(formal)
Dear Father
(religious name):
(informal)

Respectfully yours,
(formal)
Sincerely yours,
(informal)

Catholic Monsignor
(Higher Rank):

The Right Reverend
Monsignor (full
name)
(Local address)

Right Reverend and
Dear Monsignor
(surname):
(formal)
Dear Monsignor
(surname):
(informal)

Respectfully yours,
(formal)
Sincerely yours,
(informal)

Catholic Monsignor
(Lower Rank):

The Very Reverend
Monsignor (full
name)
(Local address)

Very Reverend and
Dear Monsignor
(surname):
(formal)
Dear Monsignor
(surname):
(informal)

Respectfully yours,
(formal)
Sincerely yours,
(informal)

Rector of Catholic Seminary or Head of Catholic College:	The Very Reverend (full name) (Local address)
	Very Reverend and Dear Father (religious name): (formal) Dear Father (religious name): (informal)
	Respectfully yours, (formal) Sincerely yours, (informal)
Provincials of Religious Orders:	The Very Reverend Father Provincial (Name, title of order) (Local address)
	Very Reverend and Dear Father Provincial: (formal) Dear Father Provincial: (informal)
	Respectfully yours, (formal) Sincerely yours, (informal)
Regular Catholic Clergy:	The Reverend (full name) (Local address)
	Dear Father (religious name):
	Sincerely yours,

Mother Superior of Catholic Convent:	The Reverend Mother Superior, (initials of order) Convent of (name) (Local address)
	Dear Reverend Mother:
	Sincerely yours,
Catholic Sister:	Sister (religious name plus surname) (Name of organization) (Local address)
	Dear Sister (religious name):
	Sincerely yours,
Catholic Brother:	Brother (religious name plus surname) (Name of organization) (Local address)
	Dear Brother (religious name):
	Sincerely yours,
Mormon Bishop:	Bishop (full name) Church of Jesus Christ of Latter-Day Saints (Local address)
	Dear Bishop (surname):
	Sincerely yours,

Protestant Episcopal Bishop:	The Right Reverend (full name) Bishop of (bishopric) (Local address)
	Right Reverend Sir: (formal) Dear Bishop (surname): (informal)
	Respectfully yours, (formal) Sincerely yours, (informal)
Methodist Bishop:	The Reverend (full name) Methodist Bishop (Local address)
	Reverend Sir: (formal) My dear Bishop: (informal)
	Respectfully yours, (formal) Sincerely yours, (informal)
Chaplain:	Chaplain (full name) (Rank, service designation) (Post office address of organization and station)
	Dear Chaplain (surname):
	Sincerely yours,

Army, Air Force, Marine Corps

Lieutenant General, Major General, Brigadier General, General:	(Full rank) (full name), (abbreviation of service designation) (Post office address of organization and station)
	Dear General (surname):
	Sincerely yours,
Colonel, Lieutenant Colonel:	(Same as above)
	Dear Colonel (surname):
	Sincerely yours,
Major, Captain:	(Same as above)
	Dear (rank) (surname):
	Sincerely yours,
First Lieutenant, Second Lieutenant:	(Same as above)
	Dear Lieutenant (surname):
	Sincerely yours,
Chief Warrant Officer, Warrant Officer:	(Same as above)
	Dear Mr. (surname):
	Sincerely yours,
Master Sergeant, Sergeant Major,	(Same as above)

Sergeant First Class, Platoon Sergeant, Technical Sergeant, Staff Sergeant, Sergeant:	Dear Sergeant (surname):
	Sincerely yours,
Corporal:	(Same as above)
	Dear Corporal (surname):
	Sincerely yours,
Specialist, Classes 4 to 9:	(Same as above)
	Dear Specialist (surname):
	Sincerely yours,
Private First Class, Private:	(Same as above)
	Dear Private (surname):
	Sincerely yours,
Airman First Class, Airman Second Class, Airman Third Class, Basic Airman:	(Same as above)
	Dear Airman (surname):
	Sincerely yours,
Retired Officer:	(Full rank) (full name), (abbreviation of service designation) (Local address)
	Dear (rank) (surname):
	Sincerely yours,

Navy, Coast Guard

Admiral, Vice Admiral, Rear Admiral:	(Full rank) (full name), (abbreviation of service designation) (Post office address of organization and station) Dear Admiral (surname): Sincerely yours,
Commodore, Captain, Commander:	(Same as above) Dear (rank) (surname): Sincerely yours,
Lieutenant Commander, Lieutenant, Lieutenant (jg), Ensign, Chief Warrant Officer, Enlisted Man:	(Same as above) Dear Mr. (surname): Sincerely yours,
Retired Officer:	(Full rank) (full name), (abbreviation of service designation) (Local address) Dear (rank) (surname): Sincerely yours,

Service Academy Members

Cadet, Army or Coast Guard:	Cadet (full name) (Local address) Dear Cadet (surname): Sincerely yours,
Midshipman, Navy:	Midshipman (full name) (Local address) Dear Midshipman (surname): Sincerely yours,
Air Cadet, Air Force:	Air Cadet (full name) (Local address) Dear Air Cadet (surname): Sincerely yours,

Academic Titles

President of a University or College (with Doctoral Degree):	Dr. (full name) President (Name of institution) (Local address) Dear Dr. (surname): Sincerely yours,
President of a University or College (without Doctoral Degree):	Mr. (full name) President (Name of institution) (Local address) Dear Mr. (surname): Sincerely yours,

Dean of a School (with Doctoral Degree):	Dr. (full name) Dean School of (name) (Name of institution) (Local address) Dear Dr. (surname): Sincerely yours,
Dean of a School (without Doctoral Degree):	Dean (full name) School of (name) (Name of institution) (Local address) Dear Dean (surname): Sincerely yours,
Professor (with Doctoral Degree):	Dr. (full name) Department of (name) (Name of institution) (Local address) Dear Dr. (surname): Sincerely yours,
Professor (without Doctoral Degree):	Professor (full name) Department of (name) (Name of institution) (Local address) Dear Professor (surname): Sincerely yours,
Associate Professor, Assistant Professor:	Mr. (full name) Associate (or Assistant) Professor

Department of
(name)
(Name of institution)
(Local address)

Dear Professor
(surname):

Sincerely yours,

Abbreviated Titles and Degrees

A.B.	Bachelor of Arts
Ae.E.	Aeronautical Engineer
A.F.D.	Doctor of Fine Arts
A.M.	Master of Arts
A.M.L.S.	Master of Arts in Library Science
Ar.M.	Master of Architecture
B.A.	Bachelor of Arts
B.Ag. or B.Agr.	Bachelor of Agriculture
B.Ar. or B.Arch.	Bachelor of Architecture
B.A.S. or B.A.Sc.	Bachelor of Applied Science
B.B.A.	Bachelor of Business Administration
B.C.	Bachelor of Chemistry
B.C.E.	Bachelor of Civil Engineering; Bachelor of Chemical Engineering

B.C.L.	Bachelor of Civil Law
B.D.	Bachelor of Divinity
B.D.S.	Bachelor of Dental Surgery
B.E.	Bachelor of Engineering
B.E.E.	Bachelor of Electrical Engineering
B.F.A.	Bachelor of Fine Arts
B.J.	Bachelor of Journalism
B.L.	Bachelor of Laws
B.Lit. or B.Litt.	Bachelor of Literature, or Letters
B.L.S.	Bachelor of Library Science
B.M.	Bachelor of Medicine
B.M.E.	Bachelor of Mining Engineering
B.Mus.	Bachelor of Music
B.P.E.	Bachelor of Physical Education
B.S. or B.Sc.	Bachelor of Science
B.S.Ed.	Bachelor of Science in Education
B.T. or B.Th.	Bachelor of Theology
B.V.Sc.	Bachelor of Veterinary Science
C.E.	Civil Engineer
Ch.E. or Chem.E.	Chemical Engineer
D.C.L.	Doctor of Civil Law

D.D.	Doctor of Divinity
D.D.S.	Doctor of Dental Surgery
D.F.A.	Doctor of Fine Arts
D.Lit. or D.Litt.	Doctor of Literature, or Letters
D.L.S.	Doctor of Library Science
D.M.D.	Doctor of Dental Medicine
D.Mus.	Doctor of Music
D.O.	Doctor of Osteopathy
D.P.H.	Doctor of Public Health
D.S. or D.Sc.	Doctor of Science
D.Th. or D.Theol.	Doctor of Theology
D.V.M.	Doctor of Veterinary Medicine
Ed.B.	Bachelor of Education
Ed.D.	Doctor of Education
Ed.M.	Master of Education
E.E.	Electrical Engineer
E.M.	Engineer of Mines
Eng.D.	Doctor of Engineering
F.A.C.P.	Fellow of the American College of Physicians
F.A.C.S.	Fellow of the American College of Surgeons
F.A.G.S.	Fellow of the American Geographical Society

F.A.I.A.	Fellow of the American Institute of Architects
J.C.D.	Doctor of Canon or Civil Law
J.D.	Doctor of Laws; Juris Doctor; Doctor of Jurisprudence
Jur.D.	Doctor of Law
L.B.	Bachelor of Letters
L.H.D.	Doctor of Humanities
Lit.B. or Litt.B.	Bachelor of Literature, or Letters
Lit.D.	Doctor of Literature, or Letters
Litt.D.	Doctor of Letters
LL.B.	Bachelor of Laws
LL.D.	Doctor of Laws
LL.M.	Master of Laws
M.A.	Master of Arts
M.Agr.	Master of Agriculture
M.B.	Bachelor of Medicine
M.B.A.	Master in Business Administration
M.C.L.	Master of Civil Law
M.D.	Doctor of Medicine
M.D.S.	Master of Dental Surgery
M.Ed.	Master of Education
M.L.S.	Master of Library Science

M.P.E.	Master of Physical Education
M.S. or M.Sc.	Master of Science
M.S.E.	Master of Science in Engineering
Mus.B. or Mus.Bac.	Bachelor of Music
N.E.	Naval Engineer
Pe.B.	Bachelor of Pediatrics
Phar.B.	Bachelor of Pharmacy
Phar.D. or Pharm.D.	Doctor of Pharmacy
Phar.M.	Master of Pharmacy
Ph.B.	Bachelor of Philosophy
Ph.C.	Pharmaceutical Chemist
Ph.D.	Doctor of Philosophy
Ph.G.	Graduate in Pharmacy
Pod.D.	Doctor in Podiatry
R.N.	Registered Nurse
S.B. or Sc.B.	Bachelor of Science
S.D. or Sc.D.	Doctor of Science
Sc.M.	Master of Science
S.J.D.	Doctor of Juridical Science
S.M. or Sc.M.	Master of Science
S.T.B.	Bachelor of Sacred Theology
S.T.D.	Doctor of Sacred Theology
S.T.M.	Master of Sacred Theology

Th.D.	Doctor of Theology
V.M.D.	Doctor of Veterinary Medicine

Common Abbreviations

a, amp.	ampere(s)
A-1	first-class
a.a.	author's alterations
a/c	account
A/C	account current
A/cs Pay.	accounts payable
A/cs Rec.	accounts receivable
a/d	after date
ad loc.	to or at the place
ad. val., a/v	*ad valorem* ("according to value")
a.f., AF	audio frequency
a-h	ampere-hour
a/o	account of
at. vol.	atomic volume
at. wt.	atomic weight
b.	born
bbl.	barrel(s)
B/C	bill of collection
B/D	bank draft; bar draft
B/E	bill of exchange; bill of entry
Bev.	billion electron volts
bf.	boldface
b.f.	board foot or feet
B/F	brought forward

B/L	bill of lading
B/P	bills payable; bill of parcels; blueprint
b.pay.	bills payable
B/R	bills receivable; builders' risks
B/S	bill of sale; bill of store
Bs/L	bills of lading
B/St.	bill of sight
Btu	British thermal unit(s)
b.v., B/v	bill of value; book value
c.	cent(s); carat; chapter(s)
C.	Celsius; centigrade; Congress
C/A	capital account; credit account; current account; commercial agent
C a/c	current account
c.a.f.	cost, assurance, freight
C/B	cash book
cc	cubic centimeter; carbon copy
ccm	centimeter(s)
C/D	certificate of deposit; commercial dock; consular declaration
cf.	compare
c/f	carried forward

c. & f.	cost and freight
c.f.i.	cost, freight, and insurance
cg	centigram(s)
cl	centiliter
c.l.	carload
clt., coll. tr.	collateral trust
cm	centimeter(s)
cm. pf.	cumulative preferred
cn.	consolidated
C/N	credit note; consignment note; circular note
c/o	in care of; carried over
C/O	cash order; certificate of origin; case oil
C.O.D., c.o.d.	cash, or collect, on delivery
c.o.s.	cash on shipment
C.P.A., CPA	Certified Public Accountant
CPI	consumer price index
C.P.S., CPS	Certified Professional Secretary
C.R.	class rate; current rate; company's risk; carrier's risk
c/s, cs.	cases
cu.	cubic
cu. cm	cubic centimeter(s)
cu. in.	cubic inch(es)
cu. mi.	cubic mile(s)
c.w.o.	cash with order

cwt.	hundredweight(s)
d/a	days after acceptance
D/A	deposit account; documents against acceptance; discharge afloat
db	decibel
d.b.a.	doing business as
dd.	delivered
D/d	days after date
D/D	demand draft; delivered at destination; delivered at docks; docks due
d.f.	dead freight
dg	decigram(s)
dkg	dekagram
dkl	dekaliter
dkm	dekameter
dl	deciliter
D/L	demand loan
d.l.o.	dispatch loading only
D.L.O.	dead-letter office
dm, decim.	decimeter(s)
D/N	debit note
do.	ditto (the same)
D/O	delivery order
dr.	debtor; debit; drawer
D/R	deposit receipt
D/s	days after sight
d.w.	dead weight

d.w.c.	dead-weight capacity
dwt.	pennyweight(s)
D/y	delivery
e.g.	*exempli gratia* ("for example")
e.m.p.	end-of-month payment
e.o.	*ex officio* ("by virtue of an office")
e.o.m.	end of the month (payments)
et al.	*et alii* ("and others")
et seq.	*et sequens* ("and the following")
et ux.	and wife
et vir.	and husband
ex	out of or from; without or not including
f., ff.	following (used after a numeral)
F., Fahr.	Fahrenheit
f.a.a.	free of all average
f.b.	freight bill
f.d.	free delivery; free discharge; free dispatch
fl. dr.	fluid dram
fl. oz.	fluid ounce(s)
fm.	fathom(s)
FM	frequency modulation
fn.	footnote
f.o.b.	free on board

F.P.	floating policy; fully paid
f.p.s.	feet per second
F/R	freight release
fwd.	forward
F.X.	foreign exchange
F.Y.I.	for your information
g.gr.	great gross (twelve gross)
gr. wt.	gross weight
g.s.	ground speed
HF	high frequency
Hg	hectogram
hl	hectoliter
Hz.	hertz
ibid.	*ibidem* ("in the same place")
id.	*idem* ("the same")
i.e.	*id est* ("that is")
in loc.	*in loco* ("in the proper place")
i.p.s.	inches per second
i.v.	invoice value; increased value
j.	joule
J/A	joint account
k.	carat; karat; knot
kc	kilocycle(s)
kg, kgm	kilogram(s)
kl	kiloliter(s)
km	kilometer(s)
kv	kilovolts
kv-a	kilovolt-ampere

kw	kilowatt
l	liter(s); line
L/A	letter of authority; landing account; Lloyd's agent
l.c., lc.	lowercase
L/C	letter of credit
l.c.l.	less than carload lot
lf.	lightface
l.f.	ledger folio
LF	low frequency
LL	leased line
loc. cit.	*loco citato* ("in the place cited")
log.	logarithm
long.	longitude
l.t.	long ton; local time
m	meter(s); masculine; married; minutes
M, M.	thousand; monsieur; noon (*meridie*)
ma	milliampere
m/a	my account
mb	millibar
mc	megacycle
M/C	marginal credit
m/d	months after date
mg, mgm	milligram(s)
min. B/L	minimum bill of lading
mm	millimeter(s)
M/O, M.O.	money order
M.P.	Member of Parliament;

| | military police;
mounted police |
m.p.h.	miles per hour
mr	milliroentgen
ms.(s)	manuscript(s)
M/s, m/s	months after sight
m.v.	market value
na, NA	not available
n/a, N.A.	no account
N.B., n.b.	*nota bene* ("note
well")
n.e.	not exceeding
n/f	no funds
n.g.	no good (colloquial)
NL	night letter
(telegraph)
n/o	in the name of
non seq.	*non sequitur* ("does
not follow")
n/p	net proceeds
n.p. or d.	no place or date
n.r.	no risk; net register
nt. wt.	net weight
nth	indefinite
nv	nonvoting
o/a	on account of
ob	*obiit* ("died")
o/c	overcharge(s); over
the counter
o/d	on demand
o.e.	omissions excepted
O/o	order of
o.p.	out of print

op. cit.	*opere citato* ("in the work cited")
o.r.	owner's risk
o/s	out of stock
O/S	on sample; on sale or return
o.t.	overtime
o.w.	one way (fare)
p.	page; parallel; peace
p.a.	*per annum* ("by the year; each year"); private account
P/A	purchasing agent; power of attorney
P/Av.	particular average
PBX	private branch exchange
P/C	petty cash; price current
pct.	percent
pfd.	preferred
P/N, p.n.	promissory note
P.O.D.	pay on delivery
P.O.R., p.o.r.	pay on receipt
pp.	pages
P.P.	parcel post
ppd.	prepaid; postpaid
pro tem	*pro tempore* ("for the time being")
pwt.	pennyweight
P.X., p.x.	please exchange; post exchange
q	quintal

Q.E.D., q.e.d.	*quod erat demonstrandum* ("which was to be proved or demonstrated")
q.v.	*quod vide* ("which see")
R/A	refer to accept of
R/C	reconsigned
re	about; in regard to
rev. A/C	revenue account
RF	radio frequency
rhp.	rated horsepower
rm.	ream (paper); room(s)
r.m.s.	root mean square
R.O.G.	receipt of goods
r.p.m.	revolutions per minute
r.p.s.	revolutions per second
R.S.V.P.	*Respondez s'il vous plait* ("Please reply")
rva	reactive volt-ampere
s	stere; seconds
s/a	subject to approval; safe arrival
S/B	statement of billing
S/D	sight draft
shp.	shaft horsepower
sic	so; thus (intentionally so written)
S/N	shipping note

S.O., s.o.	seller's option; shipping order; ship's option
ss	*scilicet* ("namely")
s.v.p.	*s'il vous plaît* ("if you please")
t	metric ton(s)
t.a.w.	twice a week
t.b., T.B.	trial balance
T/C	until countermanded
T/D	time deposit
tf., t.f.	till forbidden
T/L	time loan
T/O	transfer order
T/R	trust receipt
TWX	teletypewriter exchange
u.c., uc.	uppercase
ult.	*ultimo* ("of the last month")
u.s.	*ut supra* ("as above")
U/w	underwriter
v.	volt; versus
V.	value; velocity; volt
va, v-a	volt-ampere
v.f., VF	video frequency
VHF	very high frequency
v.i.	*vide infra* ("see below")
viz.	*videlicet* ("namely; that is")
vs.	versus
v.v.	vice versa

w.	watt
w.a.	with average
w/d	warranted
w.f.	wrong font (typeface)
wh, w-h	watt-hour
w.i.	when issued
w.l.	wave length
W/M	weight and/or measurement
w.o.c.	without compensation
W.R.	warehouse receipt
W.W., ww	with warrants
W/W	warehouse warrant
x-c, x-cp.	ex-coupon
x-d, x-div.	ex-dividend
x-i, x-in., x-int.	ex-interest
z.	zone; zero

Common Weights and Measures

Linear Measure

12 inches	= 1 foot
3 feet	= 1 yard
5½ yards	= 1 rod, pole, or perch = 16½ feet
40 rods	= 1 furlong = 220 yards = 660 feet
8 furlongs	= 1 statute mile = 1,760 yards = 5,280 feet
3 miles	= 1 league = 5,280 yards = 15,840 feet

6,076.12 feet	= 1 nautical, geographical, or sea mile

Area Measure

144 square inches	= 1 square foot
9 square feet	= 1 square yard = 1,296 square inches
30¼ square yards	= 1 square rod = 272¼ square feet
160 square rods	= 1 acre = 4,840 square yards = 43,560 square feet
640 acres	= 1 square mile
1 mile square	= 1 section of land
6 miles square	= 1 township = 36 sections = 36 square miles

Cubic Measure

1,728 cubic inches	= 1 cubic foot
27 cubic feet	= 1 cubic yard

Gunter's or Surveyors' Chain Measure

7.92 inches	= 1 link
100 links	= 1 chain = 4 rods = 66 feet
80 chains	= 1 statute mile = 320 rods = 5,280 feet

Liquid Measure

4 gills	= 1 pint
2 pints	= 1 quart
4 quarts	= 1 gallon = 8 pints = 32 gills
16 fluid ounces	= 1 pint

Apothecaries' Fluid Measure

60 minims	= 1 fluid dram
8 fluid drams	= 1 fluid ounce
16 fluid ounces	= 1 pint = 128 fluid drams
2 pints	= 1 quart = 32 fluid ounces = 256 fluid drams
4 quarts	= 1 gallon = 128 fluid ounces = 1,024 fluid drams

Dry Measure

2 pints	= 1 quart
8 quarts	= 1 peck = 16 pints
4 pecks	= 1 bushel = 32 quarts

Avoirdupois Weight

16 ounces	= 1 pound
100 pounds	= 1 hundredweight
20 hundredweights	= 1 ton = 2,000 pounds

| 112 pounds | = 1 gross or long hundredweight |
| 20 gross or long hundredweights | = 1 gross or long ton = 2,240 pounds |

Troy Weight

The grain is the same in all three tables of weight (avoirdupois, troy, and apothecaries' weights).

24 grains	= 1 pennyweight
20 pennyweights	= 1 ounce troy = 480 grains
12 ounces troy	= 1 pound troy = 240 pennyweights = 5,760 grains

Apothecaries' Weight

The grain is the same in all three tables of weight (avoirdupois, troy, and apothecaries' weights).

20 grains	= 1 scruple
3 scruples	= 1 dram apothecaries' = 60 grains
8 drams apothecaries'	= 1 ounce apothecaries' = 24 scruples = 480 grains
12 ounces apothecaries'	= 1 pound apothecaries' = 96 drams apothecaries' = 288 scruples = 5,760 grains

Metric Weights and Measures

In the metric system of weights and measures, names for multiples and subdivisions of a given unit may be found by combining with the name of the unit the prefixes *deka, hecto,* and *kilo,* meaning, respectively, 10, 100, and 1,000; and *deci, centi,* and *milli,* meaning, respectively, one-tenth, one-hundredth, and one-thousandth.

Linear Measure

10 millimeters	= 1 centimeter
10 centimeters	= 1 decimeter = 100 millimeters
10 decimeters	= 1 meter = 1,000 millimeters
10 meters	= 1 dekameter
10 dekameters	= 1 hectometer = 100 meters
10 hectometers	= 1 kilometer = 1,000 meters

Area Measure

100 square millimeters	= 1 square centimeter
10,000 square centimeters	= 1 square meter = 1,000,000 square millimeters
100 square meters	= 1 are
100 ares	= 1 hectare = 10,000 square meters
100 hectares	= 1 square kilometer = 1,000,000 square meters

Volume Measure

10 milliliters	= 1 centiliter
10 centiliters	= 1 deciliter = 100 milliliters
10 deciliters	= 1 liter = 1,000 milliliters
10 liters	= 1 dekaliter
10 dekaliters	= 1 hectoliter = 100 liters
10 hectoliters	= 1 kiloliter = 1,000 liters

Cubic Measure

1,000 cubic millimeters	= 1 cubic centimeter
1,000 cubic centimeters	= 1 cubic decimeter = 1,000,000 cubic millimeters
1,000 cubic decimeters	= 1 cubic meter = 1 stere = 1,000,000 cubic centimeters = 1,000,000,000 cubic millimeters

Weight

10 milligrams	= 1 centigram
10 centigrams	= 1 decigram = 100 milligrams
10 decigrams	= 1 gram = 1,000 milligrams
10 grams	= 1 decagram
10 decagrams	= 1 hectogram = 100 grams

10 hectograms	= 1 kilogram = 1,000 grams
1,000 kilograms	= 1 metric ton

Metric and Common Equivalents

Equivalents involving decimals are, in most instances, rounded off to the third decimal place except where they are exact.

Lengths

1 centimeter	= 0.3937 inch
1 chain (Gunter's or surveyors')	= 66 feet
1 chain (engineers')	= 100 feet
1 fathom	= 6 feet or 1.829 meters
1 foot	= 0.305 meter
1 furlong	= 660 feet
1 hand	= 4 inches
1 inch	= 2.540 centimeters (exactly)
1 kilometer	= 0.621 mile
1 league (land)	= 3 statute miles or 4.828 kilometers
1 meter	= 39.37 inches or 1.094 yards
1 mile (statute)	= 5,280 feet or 1,609 kilometers
1 mile (nautical)	= 1.852 kilometers (exactly) or 1.151 statute miles or 6,076.115 feet
1 yard	= 0.9144 meter (exactly)

Areas of Surfaces

1 acre	= 43,560 square feet or 0.405 hectare
1 hectare	= 2.471 acres
1 square centimeter	= 0.155 square inch
1 square meter	= 1.196 square yards
1 square mile	= 259.000 hectares

Capacities or Volume

1 barrel, liquid	= 31 to 42 gallons
1 barrel, standard, dry	= 3.281 bushels, struck measure
1 bushel (U.S.) (struck measure)	= 2,150.42 cubic inches (exactly)
1 cord (firewood)	= 128 cubic feet
1 cubic foot	= 7.481 gallons or 28.317 cubic decimeters
1 cubic meter	= 1.308 cubic yards
1 cubic yard	= 0.765 cubic meter
1 board foot	= 1 foot long, 1 foot wide, 1 inch thick
1 cup, measuring	= 8 fluid ounces or ½ liquid pint
1 gallon (U.S.)	= 3.785 liters or 0.833 British gallon
1 liter	= 1.057 liquid quarts or 0.908 dry quart
1 quart, dry (U.S.)	= 1.101 liters or 0.969 British quart

1 quart, liquid (U.S.)	= 0.946 liter or 0.833 British quart
1 tablespoon	= 3 teaspoons
1 teaspoon	= ⅓ tablespoon

Weights or Masses

1 carat	= 200 milligrams
1 gram	= 15.432 grains or 0.035 ounce, avoirdupois
1 hundredweight, gross or long	= 112 pounds or 50.802 kilograms
1 hundredweight, net or short	= 100 pounds or 45.359 kilograms
1 kilogram	= 2.205 pounds
1 pound, avoirdupois	= 1.215 troy or apothecaries' pounds or 453.59237 grams (exactly)
1 pound, troy or apothecaries'	= 0.823 avoirdupois pound or 373.242 grams
1 ton, gross or long	= 2,240 pounds or 1.12 net tons (exactly) or 1.016 metric tons
1 ton, metric	= 2,204.622 pounds or 0.984 gross ton or 1.102 net tons
1 ton, net or short	= 2,000 pounds or 0.893 gross ton or 0.907 metric ton

Kilometers to Miles

To convert kilometers into miles, multiply by 0.6 (1 mile = 1.609 kilometers).

Kilometers	Miles
1	0.62
3	1.86
4	2.48
7	4.34
9	5.58
10	6.20
15	9.30
20	12.40
40	24.80
50	31.00
60	37.20
80	49.60
90	55.80
100	62.00

Liters to Gallons

(1 gallon = 3.79 liters)

Liters	Gallons	Liters	Gallons
1	0.26	8	2.11
2	0.53	9	2.38
3	0.79	10	2.64
4	1.06	11	2.91
5	1.32	12	3.18
6	1.58	13	3.44
7	1.85	14	3.71

Liters	Gallons	Liters	Gallons
15	3.97	40	10.56
16	4.23	50	13.20
17	4.50	60	15.84
18	4.76	70	18.48
19	5.04	75	19.80
20	5.28	80	21.12
30	7.92		

Meters to Feet

(1 mile = 1610 meters)

Meters	Feet
1	3.3
5	16.4
10	32.8
20	65.6
25	82.0
50	164.0
100	328.0
161	(1/10 mi.) 528.0
500	1,640.0
805	(1/2 mi.) 2,640.0
1,000	(1 kilo.) 3,280.0
1,610	(1 mi.) 5,280.0
2,000	(2 kilo.) 6,560.0
3,220	(2 mi.) 10,560.0

Mathematical Signs and Symbols

$+$	Plus
$-$	Minus
$\times$	Multiplied by
$\div$	Divided by
$=$	Equals
$\pm$	Plus or minus
$\neq$	Not equal to
$\approx$	Nearly equal to
$>$	Greater than
$<$	Less than
$\geq$	Greater than or equal to
$\leq$	Less than or equal to
$\subset$	Included in
$\supset$	Excluded from
$\sim$	Difference
$\doteq$	Approaches a limit
$\parallel$	Parallel
$\perp$	Perpendicular to
$\therefore$	Hence
$\because$	Because
$\cdot$	Multiplied by
$::$	Proportion
$\sqrt{}$	Square root
∞	Infinity
Σ	Sum of
∂	Partial differential
$\mid$	Single bond
$\angle$	Angle
$\varnothing$	Diameter
$\leftrightarrow$	Reaction goes right and left
$\updownarrow$	Reaction goes up and down
$\int$	Integral

Common Percents and Fractional Equivalents

Percent	Simple Fractions	Decimal Fractions
20	1/5	.20
25	1/4	.25
33⅓	1/3	.333
40	2/5	.40
50	1/2	.50
75	3/4	.75
100	1	1.00

Index

A

Abbreviations: capitalization of, 191-92; common abbreviations, 319-30; postal abbreviations, 276-77; spelling of, 185-86; titles and degrees, 314-19

Acknowledgment, letter of, 228

Address, forms of: envelope, 209-10; inside address, 211; with official, professional, and honorary titles, 223-24, 281-314; with personal titles, 222-23

Addressing equipment, 148-49

Aerogrammes, 74

Agenda, 156-57

Alphabetical files, 125-26

Alphabetizing, 127-29

American Automobile Association, 164

American Society of Travel Agents, 163

Apology, letter of, 229

Appointments: calendar for, 122; handling callers with and without appointments, 38; letter about, 229; on travel schedules, 164-65

Appreciation, letter of, 229

Area codes, map of, 278-79

B

Bank accounts. *See* Records
Business-reply mail, 68–69

C

Cable letters, 88
Cables. *See* Telegraph service
Calculators, 148
Calendars. *See* Reminders
Capitalization, rules for, 191–202
Carbon paper, 105–6. *See also* Typing
Certificates of mailing, 70
Certified mail, 70
C.O.D., 71
Collection letter, 230
Commercial papers, 74
Communications, 181
Complaint, letter of, 230
Computers, 148
Confidential matters, 28
Confirmation, letter of, 230
Contacts with callers, 27. *See also* Telephone
   calls; Visitors
Copying machines, 149–50
Copyrighting, 112
Corrections. *See* Typing
Credit cards: telephone, 85; using credit cards
   for reservations, 162
Cross-references, 130–31

D

Decimal files, 126–27
Dictation: taking, 116–17; taking and typing
   minutes, 159–61; transcribing by machine, 118;

transcribing notes, 117–18; dictation while traveling, 169–70
Dictation-transcription machines, 147–48
Duplicating equipment, 150
Duties, secretarial, 22–26

E

Educational background, of secretary, 20, 23
Efficiency, office, 139–52
Equipment: addressing and mailing, 148–49; calculators and computers, 148; copying and duplicating, 149–50; dictating-transcribing, 147–48; information storage and retrieval, 150; miscellaneous office aids, 151–52; type-writers, 146–47
Etiquette, 26–29, 43, 169
Experience, secretarial work, 20
Express mail, 69

F

Fast telegram, 87
Filing: advanced storage and retrieval, 133–34; charge-out cards and folders, 132; containers and equipment, 129; cross-referencing, 130–31; indexing and alphabetizing, 127–28; microfilming, 134; preparing material for, 129–30; record retention and disposal, 133; types of filing systems, 125–26
First-class mail, 67
Follow-up, memo, 231
Follow-up systems. *See* Reminders
Forms, 144–45
Fourth-class mail, 68
Full-rate messages, 88

G

Galley proofs, 114
Geographical files, 126
Grooming, 26

I

Incoming mail. *See* Mail
Indexing, 127
Information sources: almanacs and yearbooks, 267; atlases, 267-68; biographical references, 271; books of quotations, 272-73; colleges, universities, and trade schools, 261-62; dictionaries, 266; directories and indexes, 268-70; encyclopedias, 266-67; government agencies, 259; governmental data, 274-75; industry and financial information, 273-74; local clubs and civic groups, 264; newspapers and periodicals, 270-71; research institutes, 263; style and word-usage books, 272; trade and professional associations, 260-61
Information storage and retrieval equipment, 150-51
Insurance records. *See* Records
Insured mail, 71
Internal Revenue Service, 238
Introductions: letters of, 231; making, 39-40
Investment records. *See* Records
Invitations: formal, 232; formal reply, 233; informal, 232; informal reply, 232
Itinerary. *See* Travel

L

Letters: address, forms of, 222-24, 281-314; basic letter formats, 218-21; composing letters, 224-28; envelope, 209-10; model letters and

memos, 228-35; parts of letter, 204-17. *See also* Memos
Letters and letter packages, 72-73
Local calls. *See* Telephone service
Long-distance calls. *See* Telephone service

M

Mail: annotating mail, 53; assembling mail and handling enclosures, 62-63; categories of mail, 50-51; daily register, 54-55; effective techniques, 58-60; folding and inserting mail, 64-65; getting signatures, 60-62; opening and sorting mail, 50, 52; personal and confidential mail, 51; postal information, 65-75; preparing and routing mail, 52-54, 58; sorting aids, 51; treatment of classes of mail, 56-57; when employer is away, 54-56
Mailgram, 69-70, 87
Mailing aids, 71-72
Mailing equipment, 148-49
Mathematical signs and symbols, 341
Measures. *See* Weights and measures
Meetings: duties during meeting, 157-58; preparing for meeting, 154-56; taking and typing minutes, 159-60
Memos: composing letters and memos, 224-26; memo format, 221-22; model letters and memos, 228-35. *See also* Letters
Metric weights and measures, 334-40. *See also* Weights and measures
Microfilming, 134
Money orders, 71

N

Night letter, 87
Numerical files, 126

O

Office layout, 143–44
Order, memo, 233
Ordering and requisitioning supplies, 135–36
Organizations, sources of information, 258–64
Outgoing mail. *See* Mail

P

Page proofs, 114
Parcel post, 74
Percents and fractional equivalents, 342
Personal qualities, secretary, 19–22
Planning and organizing work, 140–41
Postal Service: domestic service, 66–72; international service, 72–75; regulations, 66–75. *See also* Mail
Postcards, 73
Printed matter, 73
Printing, preparing material for, 113–14
Procedures, establishing better, 140–45
Proofreading: handling, 114–15; proofreader marks, 280–81
Publications, 264–75
Punctuation marks, 172–84
Purchasing. *See* Ordering and requisitioning supplies

Q

Qualifications, secretarial work, 22–24

R

Radio photo service, 89
Radio shore-to-ship messages, 89

Records: bank account transactions, 246–49; expenditures, 237; family financial records, 250–52; income, 240–42; life and health insurance, 253–54; property insurance, 254–56; securities transactions, 243–46; taxes, 237–42

Referrals, 40–41

Refund, travel, 163

Registered code address, 89

Registered mail, 70–71

Relationships: with assistants, 31; with employer, 29; with departments, clients, and personnel, 30

Reminders: calendars, 121–22; follow-up system, 123; tickler card files, 124. *See also* Filing

Reports, typing, 111–12

Request, letter of, 234

Requisitions. *See* Ordering and requisitioning supplies

Reservation letter, 234

Reservations. *See* Travel

Return receipts, 71

S

Second-class mail, 67

Securities transactions. *See* Records

Shortcuts, 141–42

Skills, secretarial, 19, 23–24

Small packets, 73

Special delivery mail, 70

Special handling, mail, 70

Special services, mail, 74–75

Spelling: rules of, 185–87; troublesome words, 189. *See also* Capitalization; Word division

Storage. *See* Supplies

Subject files, 126

Success, secretarial profession, 19–32

Supplies: distributing, 136; ordering and requisitioning, 135–36; storing, 137–38

Sympathy, letter of, 235

T

Tables, typing, 112–13

Taxes. *See* Records

Techniques, effective and efficient, 25

Telegraph service: automated equipment, 87–88; charges, 89–91; cost control, 93–94; domestic service, 86–88, 89–90, 92; international service, 88–89, 90–92; typing wire messages, 91–92

Telephone calls: answering and transferring calls, 44–45; courtesy with calls, 43; handling problems, 48; map of area codes, 278–79; placing local and long-distance calls, 47; screening calls, 45. *See also* Telephone service

Telephone service: answering service, 85; automatic dialers, 84; conference, appointment, and messenger calls, 81–82; credit cards, 85; Data-Phone, 86; equipment and convenience aids, 83–84; international direct-distance dialing, 79; mobile and marine calls, 80–81; picturephone, 86; speakerphone, 83; station-to-station and person-to-person calls, 77–79; switching systems, 83; Teletypewriter, 86; tie lines, 86; WATS, 85. *See also* Telephone calls

Telex, 87, 89

Thank you letter, 235

Third-class mail, 67–68

Tickets. *See* Travel

Tickler card files. *See* Reminders

Time differences: map of time zones, 278-79; telegrams and cables, 93

Transcription. *See* Dictation

Travel: foreign travel, 166-68; payments, 239; preparing itinerary, 164-66; making reservations, 162-64; travel agents, 162-63; traveling with employer, 168-70

Typewriters, 146-47

Typing: carbon copies, 99, 105-6; cards, labels, and envelopes, 100-101; corrections, 107-8; estimating copy, 97; feeding numerous sheets, 104-5; forms and ruled lines, 99-100; material for printing, 113-14; minutes, 159-61; numbers and fractions, 101-2; organizing material, 96-98; reports and tables, 111-12; spacing after punctuation marks, 110-11; special characters, 98-99; stencils and masters, 108-9; successful techniques, 96-115; telegrams, 91-92; vertical and horizontal rules, 103-4

V

Visitors: announcing and introducing, 39-40; with and without appointments, 38; callers who must wait, 37; determining reason for visit, 36; difficult callers, 41; greeting callers, 34-35; referring callers elsewhere, 40-41

W

Weights and measures, 330-33. *See also* Metric weights and measures

Western Union. *See* Telegraph service

Word division, rules for, 187-88